THE HEART CAN LIE—
BUT HANDWRITING TELLS THE TRUTH

—The size and shape of letters

—The pressure of the pen

—The length of loops

—The width of margins

These are just a few of the instantly observable
parts of handwriting that the science of
graphology uses as clues to probe the quality of
character—and that you now can use to take the
blindness out of being in love. With a wealth of
different handwriting examples (including those
of famous people), and with the wisdom and vast
professional experience of the author,
GRAPHOLOGY FOR LOVERS lets you read
the message that can spell the difference between
shattered dreams and lasting happiness.

*FRANCES ROCKWELL, who lives in
California, comes from a distinguished family
of graphologists and is one of the most respected
handwriting analysts in America today.*

SIGNET Books of Special Interest

To order these titles,

please use coupon on

the last page of this book.

Graphology for Lovers

by
Frances A. Rockwell

A SIGNET BOOK
NEW AMERICAN LIBRARY
TIMES MIRROR

NAL BOOKS ARE ALSO AVAILABLE AT DISCOUNTS IN BULK
QUANTITY FOR INDUSTRIAL OR SALES-PROMOTIONAL USE.
FOR DETAILS, WRITE TO PREMIUM MARKETING DIVISION,
NEW AMERICAN LIBRARY, INC., 1301 AVENUE OF THE
AMERICAS, NEW YORK, NEW YORK 10019.

Copyright © 1979 by Frances A. Rockwell

SIGNET TRADEMARK REG. U.S. PAT. OFF. AND FOREIGN COUNTRIES
REGISTERED TRADEMARK—MARCA REGISTRADA
HECHO EN CHICAGO, U.S.A.

SIGNET, SIGNET CLASSICS, MENTOR, PLUME and MERIDIAN BOOKS
are published by The New American Library, Inc.,
1301 Avenue of the Americas, New York, New York 10019.

First Printing, September, 1979

1 2 3 4 5 6 7 8 9

PRINTED IN THE UNITED STATES OF AMERICA

Dedication

To my parents, who were professional graphological consultants and who conducted their own graphological service long before there were any correspondence courses or classes in this subject in the United States. They were hired by industries, banks, police departments, educators, counselors, and doctors to use handwriting analysis as a diagnostic tool in solving a plethora of problems.

Both multilingual, my parents studied with the masters and were familiar with their works in French, German, and Italian. They taught me the principles of graphology as a second language in my youth so that I could help them with the mountains of mail that poured in to the several handwriting contests which they judged for the newspapers.

Acknowledgments

I wish to thank all those people whose handwriting appears in this book for the purpose of helping readers gain insights into themselves and those with whom they wish to relate.

My gratitude also goes to the master graphologists of all times whose lifelong works have made handwriting analysis the most reliable form of body language, since it is really brain language.

No one book, or even several, can be expected to make anyone proficient in this field, which requires a deep understanding of psychology and philosophy as well as experience in the complex area of social behavior. But if this study of graphology makes the reader more aware of the importance of character factors, rather than superficial physical attraction, in human relationships, it is hoped that it will contribute to happier, more fulfilling partnerships.

—*Frances A. Rockwell*

Contents

1.

Introduction

> The two sexes were made for each other and only in the wise and loving union of the two is the fullness of health and duty and happiness to be expected.
> —*William Hall*

> Engaged couples are like a couple of explorers starting off with a bagful of sweetmeats as their only provisions.
> —*Mary Borden*

What one thing—more than anything else—is responsible for success in love and marriage as well as other phases of life?

It is not, as Madison Avenue would have you believe, a mouthwash with pucker-power, a deodorant that tickles, or a miracle cosmetic, cologne, breath mint, reducing pill, vitamin, wig, or hair transplant. In fact, it is nothing controlled by *external* forces but something *within* your own power.

It is character.

Physical attractiveness may bring you and another together in a sizzling love affair or marriage, but it won't be enough to sustain the tie until your golden anniversary.

This book will teach you to X-ray through the superficial appearance of your lover to the real person underneath and to avoid disappointments such as the ones that caused cynics to write such dismal axioms as these:

> Love is the star we look up to. Marriage is the coal hole we fall into.

> He who falls in love meets a worse fate than he who leaps from a rock. —*Plautus*

> The first sigh of love is the last of vision. —*Antoine Bret*

Why do so many people suffer disappointments in love? Because, as contemporary novelist Peter de Vries said, "We fall in love with a personality, but must live with a character."

The tragedy lies in the fact that we can become so turned on by our own biological fireworks—reactions to a person's superficial attributes—that we do not learn basic character

truths and are disillusioned when they crop up later, after the
initial excitement has begun to wear off.

You wouldn't buy a house without finding out if it had hidden mortgages, liens, termites, a leaking roof, or a weak
foundation. How can you protect yourself from worse di-
sasters in a more vital emotional investment—a love affair or
marriage? How can you discover the vices and virtues of your
potential lifemate *before* leaping into a lifelong commitment?

Two thousand years ago Publius Syrus wrote: "It is *mind*,
not body, that makes relationships last."

If you want to know what kind of mind, character, personality, or "real self" is at the epicenter of your love candidate, study his or her handwriting. It is really *mind* writing,
brain writing, or *character* writing and is a dead giveaway as
to what the writer is really like and how he'll act and react in
certain circumstances. It is the printout from his or her mental
computer.

Graphology—handwriting analysis—is a valid science
devoid of guesswork, hocus pocus, occult implications, and
broad generalities. It is used throughout the literate world as a
diagnostic tool in medicine, psychology, criminology, educa-
tion, marriage counseling, vocational guidance, and job placement. More and more ads demand that your job application be
handwritten.

According to a Chinese legend, an ancient man invented
writing after noticing the tracks birds left in the sand. There's
no way of knowing whether bird scratches actually identify
specific birds, but it was soon apparent to the Chinese that a
person's handwriting does indeed distinguish him from other
human beings. So much so that Orientals have always considered handwriting a true portrait of the mind. For many
years, skill in calligraphy was a primary requirement for
Oriental brides.

You may ask what the ancient Orient has to do with today.
After all, these days relationships are freer, and people are not
so "stuck" in their mistakes. They can experiment before
making a lifelong commitment. Today we have casual live-in
lovers, non-marriages (2.6 million couples, according to the
last census), instant marriages, quickie divorces, no-fault
divorces, and even divorce without marriage!

More and more couples are avoiding the commitment to
continuity that a wedding symbolizes—elder couples for
financial reasons (social security and complications in their

wills) and younger couples for freedom. Many of them seem to agree that marriage is like ordering a meal in a restaurant and then wishing you had what someone else ordered.

But with all this freedom of life-style, we still come back to one basic truth: no matter which life-style you choose, your happiness will depend almost entirely upon compatibility. Open marriage or May–December romance, what you're looking for is a stimulating, harmonious relationship.

How can you find one? How can you tell who will be the best lover for you? Not by looks, actions, or words, which all may be camouflaging the real person you're staking so much of your life and happiness on.

"We must look *into* people as well as at them," Lord Chesterfield warned. Graphology will enable you to total up and really know the Trinity of Selfhood: the character a person shows to the world, the one he *thinks* he has, and the one he *really* has. After you have learned the principles of handwriting analysis, you can apply them to your own handwriting. Then, when you come to an understanding of your own needs, virtues, and vices, you can turn your attention toward choosing the right lover.

It isn't true that matrimony is "the high sea for which no compass has yet been invented," as Heine once wrote. There's no reason why you shouldn't be fully aware of what you're getting into.

This book will show you how you can gain insight into character through analyzing handwriting so that you will be able to chart a happier voyage in all your relationships!

Happy sailing!

Happy loving!

Happy living!

2.
The History of
Handwriting Analysis

Graphology is very *in* these days. One author even calls it "the New Science." But actually its principles have been around for thousands of years. In fact, as long as human beings have had a written language, they have been looking for the character-revealing meanings in handwriting.

Because our American roots are mostly European and we too often ignore other even older cultures, you will probably read that graphology started in Italy in the early 1600s with Alderisius Prosper's book, *Ideographia*, or Dr. Camillo Baldo's, *How to Know the Nature and Qualities of a Person by Looking at a Letter Which He Has Written*.

Actually every ancient culture in history that has produced writing has also had observant people who tried to read into a script some clues as to the character of the writer. As Alexander Pope said "the proper study of mankind is man." People always have and always will want to understand others and how they will act and react. One of the ancient sources of such knowledge was handwriting; in every literate society, there were character detectives who sought clues to personality in handwriting.

The ancient Chinese considered a person's writing "a portrait of his mind." Confucius warned, "Beware of a man whose writing sways like a reed in the wind," and philosopher-artist Jo-Hau said, "Handwriting shows us whether it comes from a vulgar or noble-minded person."

A popular proverb in both China and Japan says that "goodness and purity, as in a lovely girl, will show in the handwriting." In fact, proposals and engagements were not consummated in these countries until experts studied the calligraphy of a girl and boy to see if they suited each other. No matter how beautiful or rich a girl was, no man would court her if her writing revealed negative traits.

In the Bible there are many references to the importance of handwriting. During a royal banquet around 600 B.C. King Belshazzar of Babylon read scribbled on the palace wall the Aramaic words: *Mene, Mene, Tekel and Upharsin*. None of his wise men could interpret the meaning, so he called in Daniel, one of the Hebrew slaves in Babylon who was recognized as a handwriting expert and dream-interpreter. Daniel said it was the handwriting of the True God who had weighed Belshazzar and his kingdom, found them wanting, and would destroy them. The interpretation was so accurate that the phrase "handwriting on the wall" has come to mean impending disaster or misfortune.

There were references to handwriting in other parts of the Bible. When David gave Solomon directions for building the temple, he said, "All this the Lord made me understand in *writing by His hand upon me.*" Later the handwritings of both David and Solomon were so individualistic, recognized, and revered that Josiah reinforced his orders to the people by referring to them. He announced publicly:

> "Prepare yourselves by the houses of your fathers . . . according to the writing of David, King of Israel, and according to the writing of Solomon, his son."

Proclamations and laws were obeyed quickly when they were in the handwriting of a famous person. In the book of Ezra we read:

> The Lord stirred up the spirit of Cyrus King of Persia that he made a proclamation throughout all his kingdom and put it also in writing.

The Book of Esther tells us that King Ahasuerus:

> sent letters unto all the provinces, into every province according to the writing thereof, and to every people after their language, that every man should bear rule in his own house.

Royal orders always appeared in the king's immediately recognized writing even though he had servants and scribes to do detail work. But you did not have to be a king for your handwriting to be important. St. Matthew referred to a long-standing law when he said: "Whosoever shall put away his wife, let him give her a *writing* of divorcement." In biblical times a person's writing represented himself and was recognized as much as his physical self. This was also true in ancient Greece.

Aesop and Aristotle were among the ancient Greek intellectuals who believed in writing as an indicator of character. The latter said, "Spoken words are the symbols of mental experience and written words are the symbols of spoken words . . . Just as all men have not the same speech sounds, so all men have not the same writing." Heraclitus stated that "Man's character is his fate" and sought clues to character everywhere, even in handwriting.

In ancient Rome, handwriting analysis was quite respected. Caesar and Cicero recommended studying it to know people accurately. Historian Suetonius Tranquillus used it in his biographies of the first twelve Caesars. In his analysis of Emperor Augustus's handwriting, he observed:

> He does not separate his words, nor does he carry over to the next line any excess letters; instead, he places them under the final word and ties them to it with a stroke.

He deduced that Augustus was a very logical, straight-thinking man, which is exactly what modern graphologists would say!

Many emperors like Justinian and Nero judged people by their writing. The former considered that when people's handwritings weakened, they were too sick or infirm to be given power. Nero actually dismissed a courtier on the grounds that "his writing shows him to be treacherous."

Handwriting analysis continued to fascinate successive generations of Italians as it had their Roman ancestors. In the early seventeenth century the world's first valuable books on the subject were published in Italy. Although the tomes of Alderisius Prosper and Dr. Camillo Baldo were not the "origins" of handwriting analysis, they *were* the first to popularize the subject, eventually making it a popular pastime, and, later, a respected science throughout western Europe.

In France many brilliant students of human nature sought solutions to the riddles of character in writing and worked hard to formulate basic rules for interpreting specific signs. The most famous were Abbé Flandrin, who wrote two books that became graphological bibles, and his pupil, Abbé Jean-Hippolyte Michon who invented the word "graphology" from the Greek root-words "grapho" ("writing") and "logos" ("science of "), and who formed the world's first graphological society which was internationally active until World War II.

His pupil, Jules Crepieux-Jamin, broke away from his teacher's method of determining character by isolating signs and letters instead of focussing on the whole script. In his book, *Psychology of the Movement of Handwriting*, he also stressed the fact that handwriting reveals psychological rather than biological facts and therefore cannot be used to tell a person's sex or age. He said of Michon's emphasis on individual strokes:

> The study of the elements is to graphology what the study of the alphabet is to the reading of prose . . .

Crepieux-Jamin persuaded psychologist Dr. Alfred Binet to use graphology in his famous intelligence testing. The latter won many converts when he publicly stated that honesty and intelligence could be detected by certain signs in handwriting.

Graphology gained great favor in Germany near the end of the nineteenth century. Among those who studied it with strict scientific methods were physiology professor and child psychologist Dr. Wilhelm Preyer and psychiatrist Dr. Georg Meyer, who led experiments which analyzed the scripts of mental patients during states of elation, depression, and mania. Other medical authorities who used graphology in treating patients were Dr. Wilhelm Dorow, Dr. Emil Kraepelin, and neurologist, Dr. Pophal, all of whom considered handwriting analysis invaluable in assessing "total individuality," as well as diagnosis and prognosis.

Dr. Preyer proved that all writing is "brain writing" and "mind writing." The hand merely holds the pen and carries out the brains's orders. He was the first to show that a man who had lost all his limbs and wrote holding the pen between his teeth produced writing similar to his previous script.

Dr. Preyer's experiments have been repeated successfully many times since then. New amputees, learning to write with artificial limbs, write exactly as they did before, whereas patients with brain damage but mobile arms and hands write differently than they did before their head injuries.

A philosophical and metaphysical dimension was added to graphology by the popular philosopher Ludwig Klages. By 1896, German graphologists had formed their own society, called *Deutsche Graphologische Gesellschaft*.

By the twentieth century the popularity of handwriting analysis spread to Switzerland where Professor Max Pulver added much insight through his works which stressed spaces in writing as related to inner freedom and constraint. Dr. Albert Schweitzer used graphology in his medical treatment of patients and was a member of the honorary committee of the *Société de Graphologie de Paris*. Freud declared that there was no such thing "as a slip of the pen" and that "there is no doubt that men express their character through their handwriting."

Interest mounted in Hungary as well where a Graphological Research Institute was established in Budapest. Dr. Klara G. Roman invented a graphodyne to study the handwriting development of children in her native Hungary and later continued to spread graphological knowledge in the United States. Famous English graphologists include Robert Sandek, Hans Jacoby and E. Thorndike.

It is impossible to cite all the individual contributions as the body of information and proof burgeoned. But by the 30s there was international interest in the study of handwriting, and in most European countries artists and writers had begun to use graphology as a tool to help them in their craft.

When Gainsborough painted a portrait, he kept a letter written by the sitter pinned to his palette. Goethe collected letters and autographs of the famous people of his day because he believed that ". . . in every man's writings the character of the writer must lie recorded." Lavater, a physiognomist and theologian, was later to use Goethe's writing samples in his graphological studies to prove there are national characteristics in handwriting.

Robert Louis Stevenson actually created a character in Dr. Jekyll and Mr. Hyde who was himself a handwriting expert. In the novel, Mr. Guest is called upon to help solve the mystery of the dual personality of the humane Dr. Jekyll and the sadistically inhuman Mr. Hyde. By observing basic similarities in their writing (in spite of the different slants) he is able to prove that these two different personalities are actually one and the same.

Among the thousands of writers in the United States and abroad who studied and believed in graphology and used it to delineate character and understand people were Edgar Allan Poe, Emile Zola, Elizabeth and Robert Browning, Georges Sand, Sir Walter Raleigh, Alexander Dumas, Baudelaire, Thomas Mann, Stefan Zweig, Lion Feuchtwanger, and John Galsworthy, who wrote "as a man lives and thinks so will he write."

In the United States graphology was popularized in the newspaper columns of such outstanding pioneers as Louise Rice, Bertha Hall, and Muriel Stafford. Other early supporters included von Hagen, Leslie French, June Downey of the

University of Iowa, and Harrington Keane, who wrote under the pseudonym "Grapho."

In the 1930s the Harvard Psychological Clinic conducted significant studies, headed by psychologists Gordon Allport and Philip E. Vernon, proving that a person's handwriting is the outer expression of his inner traits and tendencies. They collaborated with experts like Robert Saudek who was editing Duke University's publication, *Character and Personality*. New findings were added by many graphologists including Joseph Zubin, Thea Stein-Lewinson, Rose Wolfson, and Ulrich Sonnemann.

Today Huntington Hartford supports the Handwriting Institute in New York, and graphology is taught at the New School for Social Research in New York and in an increasing number of other colleges and universities in the United States and Europe, including the Sorbonne in Paris and the Institute for Applied Psychology in Zurich, Switzerland. It is often offered as a credit course to help students majoring in social sciences, law, psychology, and medicine.

Most European countries were years ahead of the United States in using handwriting analysis in vocational, criminological, psychiatric, medical, and family counseling. But our country is catching up fast and so can you!

Like today's graphologists, you too can profit from the work of the giants in the field. By using the graphological knowledge gleaned from the studies and experiments of so many experts before you, you too can become a character detective. What you learn in the pages that follow can improve your relationships and your life!

3.
How to Go About It

What Graphology Can and Cannot Do

Now you are ready to learn the principles of graphology in order to discover and understand the limitations of your friends, enemies, and yourself. Before you begin, you should realize that this science, too, has its limitations.

Handwriting analysis can give you a valuable photograph of a person's inner self and show you how he will react to people and situations in life. After you have finished this book, you will realize that the pictures you have of your friends are only surface-deep and that if you want to know them intimately you should collect their pen pictures as well as photos of them.

But even after you become adept at analyzing these pen pictures, there will still be things you won't be able to tell from handwriting alone.

1. *You cannot tell the sex of the writer*.

A large, heavy handwriting that looks masculine may belong to a girl or woman who has a strong, aggressive personality. On the contrary, a small, delicate, light-pressured script that appears feminine may belong to a shy, sentimental man.

2. *You cannot tell whether the writer is popular or unpopular*.

However, the plus and minus traits may reveal the reason why the writer attracts or repels people.

3. *You cannot predict the future from handwriting*.

You can, however, discover faults and correct them, and also discover abilities you didn't know you had, which you can then develop. A happier future may inevitably result.

4. *You cannot tell a person's job or profession*.

How could you expect to? Most people are square pegs in round holes anyway. But graphology can help you decide what type of work the writer is best suited for.

If, for example, your writing shows you to be a

people-loving extrovert, you know you'll do best in a job where you're around people: saleswork, personnel, teaching, acting, etc. If, on the other hand, your writing pegs you as a meditating introvert, you'll do better at a job where you work alone: engineer, researcher, scientist, bookkeeper, or writer.

5. *You cannot tell if people are single, married, divorced, or related to each other from their handwriting.*

6. *You cannot tell the writer's chronological age.*

But you can tell his mental age, which might tell an entirely different story than the numbers on a birth certificate. A strong, bold script can be that of a vigorous, strong-minded senior citizen, whereas a teenager can write in a faint, tired, older-looking hand. This shouldn't surprise you, for aren't traits a matter of individual character and not typical of a certain age? Isn't it true that *some* young people are more mature, sophisticated, and introspective than some adults, and *some* older people may be more active physically as well as mentally than younger people? These characteristics will show up in their writing.

It is important to remember, as you begin your study of graphology, that each person is a separate individual. Even members of the same family can be extremely different from each other. Handwriting analysis will make you aware of these differences and help you to discover harmony in relationships that might otherwise be explosive or incompatible.

How to Start

First, what will you need to analyze handwriting?

1. Several sheets of plain white, unlined paper. They shouldn't be smaller than half of an 8½ by 11 sheet of typing paper, no lighter than 16-pound and no heavier than 20-pound paper.

2. Several sheets of onionskin or tissue paper.

3. A 12-inch ruler.

4. A magnifying glass. The tiniest dots, marks, or curlicues reveal important personality clues.

5. A fountain pen, if possible. Since they are rare these days, a ball-point will do. Some graphologists say that the type of pen is probably not as important as

whether it's the one the writer always uses. For example, if a person always chooses to use a fine point, it's probably because he or she unconsciously or consciously feels that it represents his or her personality.

It's better not to use a felt-tip pen or Chinese marker pencil because they produce a deceptively thick script no matter what pressure is used.

6. Several samples of the same person's script written spontaneously at *different* times and in *different* moods. Try to get from ten to fifteen lines on an unlined, unmargined page along with the writer's signature. Some graphologists ask for ten to fifteen pages and then throw away the first few, feeling that they were probably written with self-consciousness.

If you can't get different samples of the same person's writing, have him write something he likes, dislikes, or feels strongly about, in words that have both upper and lower loop letters. It's better to have him or her choose the message—one from his own subconscious or concerning his own interests. But if he asks you to suggest something, choose a simple message like: "I love summertime with all its fun-filled sports and lazy days . . . etc." until there are at least ten lines.

Begin with Yourself

This is a book about using graphology to understand your relationships—to help you determine compatibility factors in your potential friendships and love affairs. But before you can begin to understand the idiosyncracies of others, you must first become thoroughly familiar with your own.

Begin by studying several samples of your own handwriting, written at different times and preferably in ink and on plain white paper. For best results, choose samples that were written spontaneously.

Everyone has three different personalities: the one shown to the outside world; the one he or she *thinks* he has; and the one he or she *really* has. As you apply the techniques of graphology to your own handwriting you will learn the truth about your three selves and will in turn develop a happier, more integrated personality. Knowing yourself better will help you in all your potential relationships.

What you learn about yourself may surprise you. You may be a great deal better than you thought—or a great deal worse.

Most likely you will be different from your previous self-image. But if you're willing to accept the truth about your character as it is revealed in your handwriting, and if you're eager to work on your faults and make the most of your positive traits, you'll be well on the road to improving the way in which you relate to others.

To begin, examine the samples of your handwriting that you have chosen. Later on, we'll get into a more detailed analysis, but, for the moment, use the following checklist to indicate, as best as you can, the chief characteristics of your script:

1. SLANT / Forward or backward?
2. PRESSURE / Heavy or light?
3. SIZE / Large or small?
4. SHAPE / Round, angular, or mixed?
5. LEGIBILITY / Clear or confused?

Is there one feature that seems to stand out in your writing? Is it marked by its extreme forward slant or its extra-large size? Is it unusually angular? This pronounced characteristic in writing is the clue to the dominant personality trait.

4.

How Sexy Is Your Lover?

Keeping Up with the Zone(s)

The passions are the voice of the body.

—*Rousseau*

Some things are better than sex and some are worse, but there's nothing exactly like it.

—*W. C. Fields*

Man is only truly great when he acts from the passions; never irresistible but when he appeals to the imagination.

—*Disraeli*

Sexual harmony increases happiness, health, longevity, and the chances of marital success according to psychologists, counselors, clergymen, and other experts. That's why it's an important area to study before you become involved in a love relationship.

How can you really tell how each partner will act and react to the other? Certainly not by outer appearances and not by promiscuous experimentation which can destroy trust, self-confidence, and real personal satisfaction and lead to serious problems. You can't judge sexual compatibility by a one-night stand or even a honeymoon where pressures, exaggerated expectations, and pent-up emotions can produce failures in performance and lack of fulfillment for one or both lovers.

One way to avoid such disappointments is to study the clues to sexual appetites and interests in your own and your lover's handwriting.

A person knowledgeable in graphology can detect sexual hangups and sexual needs in writing. The first place to look for them is in the lower loops of such letters as f, g, j, p, and y. These can be the main sex-indicators in a person's handwriting.

All handwriting is of course composed of letters. These can be divided into three groups: the tall letters, the middle letters, and the low-slung letters.

By placing a grid, real or imaginary, over the writing, we can then see that three zones—upper, middle, and lower—are distinguishable.

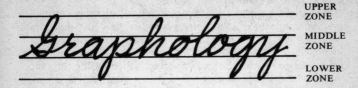

UPPER ZONE

MIDDLE ZONE

LOWER ZONE

Graphologists offer different explanations as to their meaning. Many agree with Freud and Max Pulver that the upper zone expresses the superego, the middle, the ego, and the lower, the id.

Some think of the zones in terms of a tree. Most cultures have literary references to the "Tree of Life," implying that the top of the tree, with branches lifting upward toward heaven, represents spiritual awareness. Likewise, in handwriting analysis extended upper loops (b, d, f, h, k, l, and t) are said to indicate the degree of religious, intellectual, and imaginative interests. The middle zone, composed of letters with no upper or lower extensions, is the visible trunk which stands for reality, self-interest, and contacts with others. The strength of the trunk and the visible parts of the tree depend upon the root structures beneath them.

These lower-zone letters are said to symbolize the roots of one's nature: the subconscious physical motivations for one's urges and instinctual behavior.

A theologian or religiously oriented person may think of the three zones this way:

UPPER = Heaven (the writer's spiritual, idealistic, and mental nature)

MIDDLE = Earth (the writer's realistic, day-to-day interests and relationships to others in his environment—family, friends, co-workers; not concerned with humanity in general)

LOWER = Hell (the carnal or baser materialistic emphasis including preoccupation with money, food, and the luxuries money can buy)

A girl whose head is "in the clouds" won't be happy with or make a good mate for a man whose "mind is in the gutter." A relationship may be doomed to failure if the writing in the zones is too opposite.

You don't have to condemn yourself or others if you find a predominance of one zone over another. It's just that you'll probably be happier and more sexually compatible with a lover whose loop lengths are not too different from your own. Of course sex isn't the most important aspect of life for everyone, but most experts agree that it is a vital part of a happy union, and even most non-experts agree with Reverend James R. Becherer who says, "Sex is one of the nourishments of marriage. There are people who are not talkers, not touchers, and who say openly they are not sex-minded. What right do these people have in the human relationship known as marriage?"

Whether or not you fully agree with him, you can count on the fact that if the lower loops are short, small, or nonexistent and you are looking for a sexy lover, look elsewhere. You're wasting your time with this iceberg. He or she may talk about sex a lot perhaps to mislead or arouse you, but passion isn't his or her favorite sport.

Some of the worst marriages result when a man weds a girl because he can't get her in bed any other way, only to learn that the reason she wouldn't give in before has nothing to do with virtue but is rather a lack of sex drive, which won't miraculously sprout after the minister mumbles a few words and the wedding ring is on her finger.

If you want a lover who really enjoys the full give-and-take of sex, look for someone who writes long lower loops in a right-slanted script.

while work done there no radio, no T.V., no "pleasurable?" distractions Sincerely,

If the writing slopes forward but contains large lower loops that are pulled back and slant to the left or are vertically up and down, this person's naturally strong sex drive is held in check, perhaps sublimated in work or fantasies. The pulled-back lower loops in a right-leaning script may mean occasional frustration, impotence, or frigidity in someone who seems warm and friendly—at least out of bed. But in the sack it's a different story!

Long lower loops with broad bottoms that look like "moneybags" often mean an exaggerated concern with money. In a narrow script, it warns of a Scrooge—a selfish miser. In a broad, large writing with ample margins, it could mean someone who flashes and squanders money in a bid for showing off and ego gratification, someone who tries to "buy" love and make an impression through extravagant spending instead of through worthwhile actions.

Karen, a young divorcee with two little boys, met Vince in business management class at a night school. He attracted her attention because of his clean-cut, Scandinavian good-looks, his neatness (he always wore a clean white shirt, whereas other men came to school in T-shirts and sweaters), and his love of children. Soon he was coming to her house to fix everything from the TV to the plumbing, and he played baseball, soccer, tennis, and football with the boys.

Knowing a smattering of graphology, Karen considered his large, right-slanting script with its long lower loops as an indication of passion and athletic ability. This was true, but incomplete. She was to learn the truth about him when suddenly one day he disappeared, leaving behind him a pack of creditors! Later she was shocked to find that he owed thousands of dollars to stores where he had bought gifts for her and her boys, to the IRS, to gambling casinos where he tried to earn quick money to pay his debts. (He even charged $2,000 to her credit cards.) His moneybags lower loops proved him to be the kind of person who used money to buy whomever and whatever he wanted. Sure, the elongated loops indicated athletic prowess both in bed and in sports, but the wide-bottomed loops should have warned her that he was the kind of lover who could make her miserable emotionally and bankrupt her financially.

Watch out for moneybags!

Here are samples from two different people with the same name and the same admiration for financial success. The heavier script is that of a coarser, completely material person; the other shows more culture and sensitivity but equal preoccupation with money:

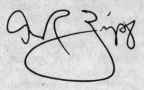

Not that moneybags are always bad. They can indicate an ability to handle finances, as in the signature of this banker:

Here's another example of a financial wizard who likes money for the luxuries it can buy, not just for himself and his family but also for others. Furthermore he doesn't want anything he doesn't earn. Superb constructive ability and originality show in the connected words "If there," "for you," "and I," "to serve," "to you," and in his signature.

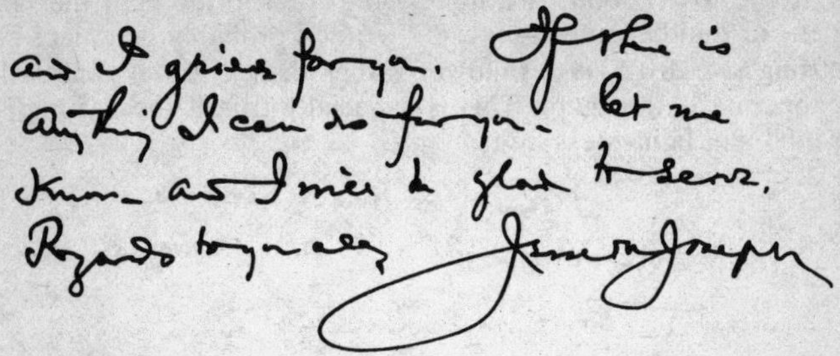

[handwritten sample]
as I grieve for you. If there is
anything I can do for you. let me
know as I will be glad to serve.
Regards to your wife, *[signature]*

Long, graceful loops in a rhythmically coordinated handwriting indicate athletic ability. Here is an illustration from the
pen of a male dancer and choreographer:

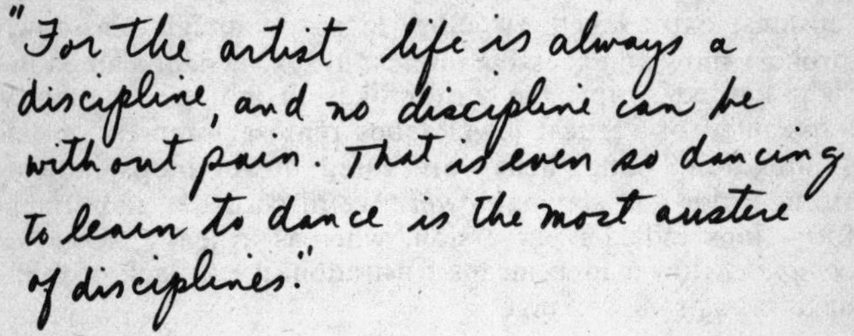

[handwritten sample]
"For the artist life is always a
discipline, and no discipline can be
without pain. That is even so dancing
to learn to dance is the most austere
of disciplines."

Sometimes a writer uses long, straight downstrokes instead
of loops. In a primitive script, thick, heavy strokes mean
cruelty, but in a cultured writing like the following, they
indicate good judgment, intelligence, and concern with basics.
If the letters look like numbers ("7" or "9" as here) the writer
has mathematical ability.

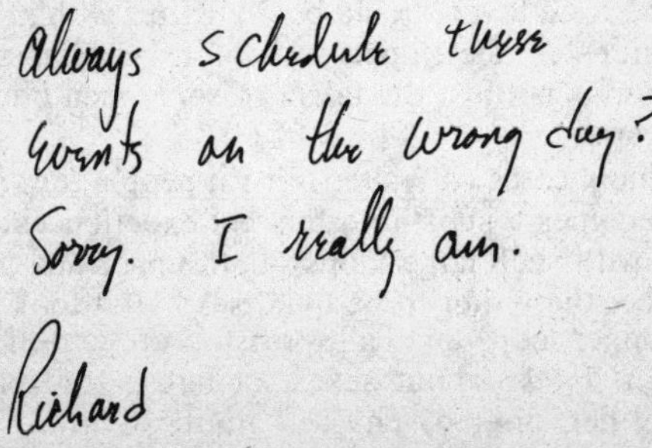

[handwritten sample]
Always schedule these
events on the wrong day?
Sorry. I really am.

Richard

If the lower loops are nonexistent or shorter than the upper - or middle-zone letters, the writer's probably lazy, lacks a strong sex drive, is a follower rather than a leader, and will cooperate with others. This is especially true if the writing is round and light-pressured.

I shall be leaving here shortly; but shall be back in Pasadena

I print much faster than I write, and think it looks neater.

To sum up the sex signals you can read in the lower extensions: extra length (whether loops or straight-line downstrokes) show an excessive interest in sex. If right-slanted in a right-slanted script, the writer likes to indulge frequently; left-slanted or vertical lower loops represent repression and sublimation. Long, heavy-pressured, lower loops indicate strong ardor and staying power. Weird curlicues and strange formations indicate perversion, whereas a heavy, large, *incompleted* lower loop means frustration due to lack of fulfillment of a strong sex urge.

UPPER ZONES (f, h, k, l, t, b, d)

The upper zone represents the world of the intellect, ideals, imagination, pride, and the superego. If upper loops and capitals are much larger than lower loops, the writer is more intellectual and spiritual than physical. He may be visionary and idealistic—especially if the writing is fine, light, and clear. Your choice for a lover should be the writer with at least *some* tall extensions in the upper zone, for, as Emerson wrote, "Imagination is not just the talent of some men but the health of every man."

We all know cases of Walter Mittys, people for whom a fantasy life becomes a substitute for real experiences. Following is a script with such large loops—both upper and lower—that you'd expect the writer to be quite sexy. But look again. The extra tall upper loops and light pressure tip you off to the fact that this girl *thinks* about sex a lot but is too religious and moral to let herself enjoy physical gratification.

I'll be back as soon as I gain enough strength for a long day. I miss you.

The taller the upper loops are, the more visionary and idealistic the writer is. He's also likely to be superstitious and "out of this world." Some scribblers with ultra-high upper loops and capitals are aptly described by the ancient Chinese proverb: "The fool reaches for the stars and forgets the flowers at his feet."

I vary my W's. Sometimes I write "H" & sometimes "W." My "E's"

Very short upper loops show that the writer has little imagination, adventure, or aspiration but is down-to-earth. He'll never let his mind soar into the stratosphere of fantasy.

clue from last nights discussion of poetry

Shortly after my husband died of cancer, when the thing I had feared had finally happened, I captured my feeling in this poem:

A good balance between upper and lower loops indicates a well-balanced character. If both upper and lower loops are inflated, the person is vital, versatile—with many interests and abilities. A large, right-slanted script, in which all loops are large, belongs to someone who's "on the ball"—ambitious, magnetic, extroverted, life-and-luxury-loving, dynamic, dramatic, and socially oriented. He or she likes to make a good impression on others and live on a high scale of grandeur and importance. No matter what his or her chronologic age, the personality will always remain youthful and attractive.

If all loops are long but the uppers are much taller than the lowers, the writer has such a highly developed intellectual, spiritual, and imaginative sense that no matter how much he or she talks about sex, the execution is more likely to be on an idealized romantic rather than physical plane.

On the other hand, the person whose upper loops are tall but not as extended as the lowers may enthrall you with a line of idealism and romantic love but is chiefly interested in satisfying his or her erotic urges (preferably first). Several "spiritual leaders" like Henry Ward Beecher and the fictional Elmer Gantry were convincing ministers but also frequently functioning Casanovas.

MIDDLE ZONES (a, c, e, i, m, n, o, r, s, u, v, w, x)

In most cases the general size and shape of the middle-zone letters are formed by the age of twelve. From then on, most major handwriting changes occur in the upper and lower zones. As teenagers develop more interest in all kinds of physical activity (including, of course, sex), the lower loops grow larger or longer. As their mental and philosophical interests increase, the upper loops also grow bigger. Later on in life, as people are less active physically, their lower loops become smaller.

Some writings emphasize the middle zone with little or no extensions into the upper or lower zones. This indicates a self-concerned person who is absolutely confident and totally interested in the humdrum events of everyday life and probably can't be pulled away from practical goings-on into a romantic or spiritual adventure. If you're an imaginative, physically and mentally active go-go dynamo, and you do get emotionally involved with this middle-zone stresser, you'll eventually be bored by the dull chitchat and exaggerated concern for nonessentials.

The middle-zone emphasizer lacks the imagination of writers with towering upper loops and the physical drive and sex interest of those with plummeting lower zones. He is more interested in himself than in anyone or anything else.

If the e's and r's are larger than the other middle-zone letters, the person cares more for clothes and personal appearance than sports or philosophy. This is the pragmatic, no-nonsense realist who lives in the here-and-now, has poise and social confidence, and wants to be in the spotlight, admired by "the right people." This person doesn't really enjoy athletics or religious activities. Perhaps he or she would be more popular if he did. At least he'd have more interesting things to talk about other than himself or those connected with him.

In a balanced personality, the mental and physical natures are not in conflict. The following writer does not feel the need to choose between spiritual and erotic urges. In his writing, upper, lower, and middle zones are equally proportioned.

> You have a hang-up if.....
>
> You find a black lace night gown in your boy friend's apartment and he tells you it's his mother's
>
> And you believe him.

And still other samples of writing by people who have achieved a felicitous balance between intellectual and physical interests and activities appear below. Notice, too, the regularity in the scripts, which makes them dependable, non-neurotic friends, companions, and/or lovers:

> Dear Mrs Rockwell,
>
> I just wanted to write and say thank you for a most enjoyable semester. You are one of the most colorful ~~enb~~ instructor I have ever taken.

> *Mrs. Rockwell,*
>
> *Happy New Year! and I hope your holiday was enjoyable. Unfortunately, I shall not be with you during the month of January.*

Now let's have a look at some handwriting samples of compatible couples, to see how sexual rapport shows up in the writing. In the tradition of "Ladies first" the woman's script precedes the man's.

> *I am truly enjoying your writing class, and although time is at a premium at the moment, I feel I am learning so much that will be of value to me in the future, when I have more time to devote to my writing. I know I'll greatly profit from it! Thank you so much for the privilege of working with you.*
>
> *Sincerely*

Good morning, It's Monday and the sun is brightly shining; let's hope that everything is going to turn out sunny and bright

This writing indicates passion (healthy, lower extensions), warm-hearted affection, and genuine interest in people (rightward slant). She is a logical planner (all letters are connected without lifting the pen) who is realistic in her dealings with people (large middle-zone letters) and who has great pride and self-confidence (large capital letters, especially "I"). Although she has a strong libido, she saves her love for *her* man only (occasionally a lower loop is incompleted, such as "truly," "greatly," or even very small as in "profit").

Her lover is equally ardent but more romantic (completed lower extensions in a writing that slants more to the right than hers). He is optimistic (uphill baselines) and extremely intuitive (wider spacing between letters and words). Whereas her interests are predominantly practical and social, his are more on the intellectual side (his middle-zone letters are smaller than hers).

This pragmatic realist and inspirational idealist complement each other well as long as they understand and accept their differences. She's an actress and he's a talented musician. But whereas she likes to be onstage in a stellar role, he doesn't need to be the soloist. In fact, he plays well with others but sometimes likes privacy (wide "don't-fence-me-in" spaces between words). Both writings show ardor (long lower loops and right slant), geniality (rounded forms), and cultural interests (some g's are like 8's).

a fun thing for me. Puzzles, equations — what have you — and tests? I thrive on tests!

[handwritten sample:] Republican by choice — an accountant by profession. I have been married to Sue for almost twenty-one years

In the second sample, the wife's graceful garland connections and emphasis on the middle-zone letters indicate graciousness, love of social activities, practicality, and amiability. Her lighter pressure means that she lets her ardent, sentimental (heavy pressure, extreme right slant) husband take the lead. Both of them like people, but, like most women, she excels in establishing and maintaining their social relationships. She is more expressive and outgoing and has excellent taste in clothes (the small e's and r's are pronounced).

Each has a sense of humor, a great enjoyment of life, and intelligence, although he is more likely to retire to reading, cultural TV programs, and his own thoughts, while she tends to practical matters.

[handwritten sample:] You will see from the enclosed I had already written a sample for you! Holding it up so Gene to add his!

Carol

[handwritten sample:] Dear Frances, Carol asked me to give you a sample of my handwriting — since I know this is

This woman and man are equally affectionate and emotional (similar extreme right slant). They also share mutual qualities of executive leadership, brain power, and the ability to concentrate (small, clear script). They are so cheerful and optimistic (uphill baselines and terminals) that nothing keeps either one down for long. The husband's logical thought processes benefit from flashes of inspiration and intuition (breaks in "Dear," "Frances," "asked," and "handwriting"). The wife's keen business acumen is enhanced by a good imagination (high t-bars) and self-confidence (underscored signature). Although she's a petite, charming Southern belle, she's also shrewd and hardworking and can hold her own in a man's world.

> *I got the Crisis-aworked out and inserted it in the story. Hope it is ok.   Dan is home and it is martini time. He had a long and busy day too.*

> *Driving the freeway every evening is not a relaxing way to finish a busy day. Sometimes it produces more tension than an eight hour workday.*

This wife is the perfect cheerer-upper for a pragmatic, sometimes moody (baselines and slant are not consistent) husband. She's more logical (small, connected letters) and he's more impulsive (space breaks between letters) and he needs her keen sense of order, whereas she can learn how to relax from him! They complement each other well.

Now let's look at some samples of incompatible couples. In no way could the following men and women ever be happy together no matter what attracted them to each other in the first place.

First, the inhibited, holier-than-thou, puritanical prude and the extroverted, passionate man with total love in his heart, soul, and body:

> *Those values which I grew up with and which I value above all others are those of honor, duty, personal integrity — and above them all valor and courage of conviction.*

> *Today is Monday*

The sensitive, sentimental, music-and-literature-loving girl with a delicate sense of humor and altruistic sense of humanity and the crude, vulgar show-off who shows no subtlety or sensitivity because he's so wrapped up in himself:

[handwritten:] Writing for me, I'm afraid, is going to be like the "other woman." when our figures were finally matched— her ego turned out to be more shapely than mine.

[handwritten:] Very busy — Obes Obe brevity.

The frigid, hypercritical, arrogant snowlady and the shy but affectionate, life-and-people-loving artist (she was his physically attractive model):

[handwritten:] Dear Alicia, As time is short, just a few lines.

[handwritten:] so unhandy. and I know I missed some sales as the location was awkward to get to. I will leave my big press there for awhile untill I can make room for it in the new place

Remember sex appeal isn't just the widest smile or the best body or the whitest teeth; instead of judging others by their super looks, look to handwriting for the deep-down truth!

5.
What Is Your Lover's Staying Power? Energy? Passion?

What You Can Tell from the Pressure

Passion, though a bad regulator, is a powerful spring.

—Ralph Waldo Emerson

Passions are like storms which, full of present mischief, serve to purify the atmosphere.

—Alan Ramsey

The passions are the winds which fill the sails of the vessel; they sink it at times, but without them it would be impossible to make way.

—Voltaire

A genuine passion is like a mountain stream; it admits of no impediment; it cannot go backward; it must go forward.

—Christian Bovee

When he was ninety-five years old, the late conductor Leopold Stokowski was interviewed by a reporter less than half his age. The young man asked him, "What is the most important thing in music and art?" His quick response was: "Passion. Without it you wouldn't be here and neither would I!" He was merely agreeing with what Balzac said over a century before: "Passion is universal humanity. Without it religion, history, romance, and art would be useless."

How can you tell whether your potential lover has it? Assuming he or she is not the world's greatest artist or musician, how can you tell whether the flow of hot-blooded passion runs through his or her veins? Because your lover writes you songs, poems, and love letters does not necessarily mean he or she is a passionate, vital bed partner. By the same token, the lack of these testimonials does not mean your partner has no staying power.

29

To judge the degree of passion and vitality, we must look further than the zones of the previous chapter. Accentuated lower-zone letters in your lover's handwriting may mean he or she is a sexual athlete, dextrous and knowledgeable. But if this keen interest isn't accompanied by endurance and strength, he or she will fizzle out, not just in the romance department but also in active participation in life, sports, travel, parties, and whatever else you may feel makes the difference between dynamic living and humdrum existing.

On the other hand, if you're a low-key person who *likes* to lead a relatively quiet life, you won't be happy with a hyperkinetic dynamo, nor will you probably want to be left alone while he or she engages in the activities that bore you with someone else.

To detect your partner's personal energy level, simply study the pressure of the writing. It will tell you how vigorously he or she reacts to people and environments. It will also reveal his or her degree of strength, endurance, intensity, fearlessness, ardor, and capacity for visualization. You will be able to avoid mismatches if you choose a lover whose script isn't too different from your own in thickness and pressure.

In evaluating pressure you must avoid two mistakes:

1. Don't underestimate the importance of the pen used. If a weakling uses a thick, black felt-tip pen, he'll produce a heavy script, whereas if a powerful person uses a light fine-point pen, his writing will look weak. If you have any doubts, turn the paper over—heavy pressure makes ridges on the back, no matter what type of pen is used.

If you are obtaining a handwriting sample, ask the person to use the kind of pen he always uses. Unconsciously he'll choose one he prefers because it expresses himself. Even if someone isn't conscious of being graphologically examined, he usually considers his handwriting an extension of himself and uses typical, revealing tools.

2. Don't consider heavy-pressured writing as proof of physical strength and think that a guy who writes a thick, dark script is a super-muscleman, while one who writes lightly is a weakling.

Graphologist Klara Roman analyzed the handwritings of tough, delinquent girls who had committed violent crimes and discovered to her amazement that they wrote much more faintly than normal, active high school girls. Hans Jacoby also found the writings of strong factory workers who performed ultramuscular tasks to be average rather than heavy-pressured.

Does that mean a thick script written with strong pressure does not indicate power and energy? Not at all. It does show vitality and strength, but it could be mental or psychic rather than physical. Remember we said that writing is *mind* writing and *brain* writing, not just motor activity! So it is, and a vital brain that is strongly motivated will express itself in a vigorous writing, whereas a physically strong brute who is lackadaisical, maladjusted, frustrated, or unmotivated to purposeful activity may write with a weak or average pressure.

Heavy pressure, therefore, indicates energy, endurance, fearlessness, robustness, vitality which may be of a creative nature rather than sheer brute force. It's this high-voltage person who gets the greatest charge out of life.

Here's the writing of a leading fantasy writer and poet of boundless energy and accomplishment. He has more physical drive and creative power than most people and therefore electrifies his readers with his contagious enthusiasm and colorful writing.

> "All this being true," the old
> man said, "if I am a good man,
> and good I think myself,
> why am I not happy?"
> To which the Demon replied,
> "Since when has goodness
> had anything to do with
> Happiness!?"
>
> Ray Bradbury

The thick writer is primarily concerned with reality and the world of the senses. He loves colors, sounds, tastes, and good smells. He loves the great outdoors. He loves life and he loves love! He is adventurous, has healthy appetites, and lives on all cylinders. He likes to work with his hands and is a doer rather than a dreamer.

Heavy Pressure - Dynamic Vitality.
realism, materialism, force,
Passion, aggression, determination

See how creative power seems to leap off the page in the scripts of geniuses like Nobel Prize-winning physicist Niels Bohr and composer Ludwig van Beethoven. The latter's vigorous writing almost makes you hear his powerful music.

Niels Bohr

L. V. Beethoven

Note the heavy pressure in the following handwriting. The writer is an artist who is visually oriented, has a marvelous sense of color and composition, and lives life with gusto.

Northridge is the opposite of
sensitivity. By this, I mean
that Northridge as an environ-
ment which nurtures the sensitive
soul of the artist is nothing but
a desert.

If the horizontal strokes are heavier—especially the t-crosses and connecting strokes—the writer has invincible willpower and a vital, vivacious personality to which other people quickly respond. If these strokes are conspicuously heavy, the writer is domineering, with a strong desire for gratification. This sign in well-formed writing indicates leadership—a person who wants to be boss and live luxuriously and who is capable of achieving this goal. Strong horizontal strokes in a heavy writing that is blurred and muddy indicate brutality. This person can be insistent upon getting his way!

Heavier vertical than horizontal strokes belong to a person who secretly yearns to be the kingpin, but who lacks the aggressiveness and leadership to follow through. This is the ambitious bluffer whose bark is worse than his bite.

In a writing that is rhythmic, well formed, and cultured, shaded vertical strokes can mean musical ability.

The person who writes with consistently heavy pressure has strong vigor, vitality, and a love of sensory stimuli and material things as well as psychic energy and an intense feeling about life. This holds true regardless of the size, slant, or shape of the script, so you must take into account the traits discussed later on in Chapters 6, 8, and 9.

Here are some samples of heavy-pressured writings, both large and small:

This energetic young lady is a tournament tennis player.

Here is an active artist, school nurse, community leader as well as an efficient

wife and mother. Her energy
level enables her to wear
many hats and get things
done!

was built in 1910 and for $15 a night for two
all meals are served. I just had French toast
this morning and am writing this note before
leaving on the drive back to L.A. Though the
jaunt was sudden, I'm enjoying it a lot. Rain,
rain both ways, but it makes the car run
better.

This is more of a mental
high-energy man who never
seems to tire. He prefers to
direct his vitality to intellectual rather than athletic pur-
suits.

A very light-pressured writing indicates sensitivity,
idealism, and more spirituality than materialism (especially if
the upper loops and strokes are high). This person is easily in-
fluenced by others and would "rather switch than fight." He's
a follower rather than a leader. If the t-crosses are very faint,
the person has practically no willpower or may tire easily.
(That's why you try to have several samples written at different times so that you're not misled by temporary traits or
moods.)

Most light-pressured writers tend to be introverts, especially
if the script is vertical or backhand. Light writing that slants to
the right indicates a person who appears shy and withdrawn
but has a great need for love and is very sensitive.

Some rainy afternoon, many years from now, a
little girl will ask her mother, what was it like
when your grandmother was alive -- what was she like?
I hope that the things I write through the years
will be an answer in the search for a family identity.

Light pressure in a rounded script denotes unselfishness, tender-loving-care, maternalism, and lack of aggressiveness. With original formations it indicates imagination, idealism, high intelligence, and aspirations.

Light-pressured writing with an unsteady baseline shows lack of confidence. With irregularity in slant and size it means instability, whereas in a regular writing it indicates an aesthetic, idealistic nature.

The writer who produces a medium pressure isn't as aggressive, sensual, or materialistic as the heavy writer or as sensitive and spiritual as the light writer. His interests are usually divided between things and people. With corroborating signs of geniality, he is the easiest person to get along with.

> *store and buy some watermelon*
> *and ice cream with cream*
> *cheese and soda crackers with*
> *only thirty-five seconds to go*

Here is the writing of a spiritual leader who is a perfect example of moderation. He is dependable, practical, clear-thinking, loves people, and understands and gets along well with them. The pressure, slant, and size are all medium and well balanced, as is he.

> *condolence in the severe loss you and*
> *yours have suffered in the sudden*
> *demise of your father. Yet it is great*
> *comfort to know what splendid*
> *character he possessed, and that his*
> *ripe old age itself as well as the*
> *family he reared speak very well*
> *for him indeed. I hope that God*
> *will have mercifully opened for*
> *him the gateway into a better life.*
>
> *Very sincerely yours*
> *Dionysius Engelhard O.F.M.*

Suppose the pressure is uneven with heavy and light alternating seemingly without rhyme or reason? This person has emotional problems, with fluctuating moods. You can get fouled up if you become too emotionally involved with him or her. Uneven pressure in youth indicates that the true character is not yet formed, but in adulthood it means that the writer is ultra-sensitive, immature, indecisive, or irritable. It also means that this person's stamina comes and goes.

> I would like to know what
> handwriting analysis might reveal
> about me.
>
> and direction.
> I can't ask you to forgive
> me for my blundering is inexcusable.
> Much love,

To judge the degree of passion that is desirable in your partner, first have an honest look at yourself. Does your handwriting reveal you to be a hot-blooded, active type? Or are you more of a shrinking violet, preferring peace, quiet, and solitude, but few pressures? Are you in the pro-passion camp with Chatfield, who wrote, "Were it not for the salutory agitations of the passions, the waters of life would become dull, stagnant and as unfit for all vital purposes as those of the Dead Sea"? Or do you agree with disbelievers like Cicero, who said, "He only employs his passion who can make no use of his reason."

Remember, there is no right or wrong here, no value judgment. We're not advocating passion or praising the lack of it. We're merely asking for an honest evaluation—one that will help you to find your most suitable mate.

6.
How Sympathetic Is Your Lover?

What You Can Tell from the Slant

Sentiment is the poetry of the imagination.
> —*Alphonse de Lamartine*

A sympathetic heart is like a spring of pure water bursting forth from the mountain-side.
> —*Anon*

If there were less sympathy in the world, there would be less trouble in the world.
> —*Oscar Wilde*

Self-control is only courage under another form.
> —*Samuel Smiles*

If you can command yourself, you can command the world.
> —*Chinese saying*

He that ruleth his spirit is better than he that taketh a city.
> —*Proverbs XIV:32*

The way a writing slants—to the right, the left, or not at all—tells whether the writer leans toward or away from people, is independent or dependent, is an extrovert, introvert, or ambivert.

The right-leaning writer is usually ruled by his emotions; the left-slanting writer is ruled by his mind; upright script indicates a logical person who is balanced—giving precedence to neither head nor heart.

Some graphologists label the left slant "defiant," the right slant "compliant," and the vertical script "self-reliant." They even go so far as to tie up these tendencies with the terms "the Right" (supporters of the Establishment), "the Left" (those who defy and challenge traditions and the status quo), and "the Middle-of-the-Roaders." It's an interesting theory and you might try it out on the writings of people you know. Does your nonconformist friend's script bend backward defiantly? Does your follower friend's scribble slant forward as if following a parade?

The best way to gauge a person's emotional attitudes through his writing is to draw the following peacock's tail-spread diagram with a heavy pen or pencil on onionskin paper. Use a ruler to make the lines absolutely straight.

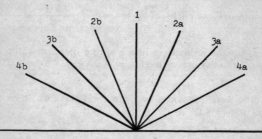

Place thin paper over the writing you are analyzing to see if the slant is closest to 1, 2a, 3a, 4a, 2b, 3b, or 4b.

The right-slanting writings from moderate (2a) to extreme (4a) indicate friendliness and extroversion, and are what Dr. Alfred Adler probably had in mind when he wrote "Handwriting points the way from me to you."

2a is the most frequent slant and fits the most "normal" temperaments. This is the writing of a school principal whose genuine sympathy and interest in others makes him popular with everyone he works with: teachers, students, clerks, and administrators. Because of his genial personality plus his abilities, he keeps climbing to higher positions in the school system.

You teach brilliantly. I wish I had time to enjoy more of your stimulating lectures

Just great!

3a is even more affectionate. This person is a good mixer who needs people and doesn't like to be alone. To her, happiness is being popular. She is subjective and future-oriented.

The following 3a slant was written by a sensitive, sentimental teenage girl. She reaches out to people with genuine affection, often wearing her heart on her sleeve. Even though she has artistic talent, true happiness will never come from a career alone but rather from being loved by the person she loves.

Roses are red,
Violets are blue.
If you can get my father
To write something,
Congratulations to you!

The emotions of the person who writes the 4a slant are even stronger, often running away with him or her. If the script leans so far to the right that it almost falls flat on its face, the writer can easily become hysterical and unbalanced, quick to make a scene. In trying to make people like or love him this eager beaver can scare them away like a scalding, erupting volcano. Don't trifle with this person's affections. You could be awfully sorry!

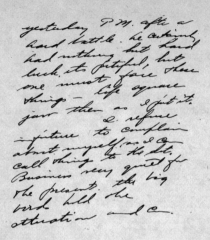

Just as a rightward slant indicates the outgoing, demonstrative nature of the extrovert, the left or backward slant reveals the withdrawn, hard-to-know personality of the introvert.

The backward-slanting writer prefers ideas, thinking and reading, or perhaps being with a very few selected friends to extensive partying and socializing. He is more of the intellectual type—the thinker rather than the doer—especially if his left-slanting script is small and clear. This type of writing denotes marvelous powers of concentration and a great ability for detail work. But if both capitals and the body of the writing are exceptionally small, the writer may be painfully modest and shy, ever afraid to join in the fun.

Before drawing conclusions, find out if the writer is left-handed, since most southpaws write backhand and therefore the introverted traits do not necessarily apply. Lord Nelson wrote right-handed until he lost his right arm at Trafalgar. Then he trained himself to write with his left hand and his script changed from right to left slant although his character did not.

In a normally written script the degree of the leftward slant corresponds with the degree of introversion—the more the script bends to the left, the more withdrawn the person is. (Many teenagers who prize their privacy or who are in a mood of rebellion against authority affect a backward slant during this period of their lives.)

2b is a mild left slant. This person isn't easy to know but is very loyal once you become his or her friend. He is selective, choosing quality rather than quantity in his acquaintances, is dependable and a down-to-earth realist.

> As soon as the envelope was sealed, it dawned on me that you intended this space for a sample of handwriting. Talk about

3b is more inhibited than 2b, shying away from people, especially crowds. Of course he has feelings—everyone has—but you'd never know it! He also may be inclined to live in the past, an inclination that increases as the writing slants more to the left.

> Hi - Nice to talk to you - Sorry about N.K.K. - (no Xmas card, German style) but I only wrote 2 + forgot to mail those - So please accept this as belated New Years greeting + wishes Fondly

Or he may shy away from the outside world, preferring the comfort and securities of family life. Below is the writing of a charming, capable woman whose social activities are all family-oriented:

for the party But after the U.S. meeting, our car smelled of gas— I took it to the car 'doctor who had to perform surgery on a

4b, the extreme left slant, indicates a very frustrated, inhibited person who denies himself emotional outlets. Sometimes there is a strong distrust of people (perhaps based on bitter experience) or even a fear of the future.

Andy—

Best of health, happiness, and success in 1979 — and in that order too!

A heavily written left slant with sharp, angular letters indicates someone who is only interested in people as a means to an end. If the middle-zone letters are emphasized with short upper loops the writer is selfish and materialistic. A girl who writes this way may prefer rich older men who can lavish luxuries on her.

The upright slant belongs to a reliable, realistic, logical person who doesn't take wild chances and is always in control of his emotions. This is "Old Faithful," the person you can count on—who won't let you down or sweep you off your feet or freeze you out!

Unlike the person with a strong left slant who tends to live in the past, or the right-slanted person, who usually lives in the future, the vertical writer lives in the present—the here-and-now.

Here are some samples of vertical writing:

Traveling is a broadening experience for one and all. Writing is very hard for me since I like to print.

I trust this book will be of great interest to you, as it shows the way into the new Aquarian Age. These are the matters that occupy most of my time these days and are most enlightening.

No matter which way the writing slants, if it's consistent, as in the following sample, the writer has willpower and is mature.

shot over the enemy's vital target for a happy Christmas evermore.
Well—way back in the year's "B.C."—they never heard about television, satellites, or Christmas—

On the other hand, changing slants in the same writing sample may indicate weak will, inconsistency, lack of discipline, vacillation, or immaturity. You never know what mood this next writer will be in or what inner conflicts he is experiencing. If you choose him as your mate, be prepared for a life full of surprises.

Dear Frances:

The following writing shows how confusion (indicated by the mixed slants) can put the brakes on creative ability. Logic is indicated in the connected letters, and imagination and inspiration in the high t-bars: but more discipline is required for assured success.

> My Bump of Outrage
> I get these brilliant flashes
> In the middle of the night;
> Get up and write my brainstorms out;
> My fancy taking flight.

If, however, the every-which-way script is remarkably clear, brilliant, and written on an absolutely straight baseline, the writer is extremely versatile. He may even be a genius, and geniuses are fun (though they can be exhausting!).

A person who writes different slants at different times but maintains the same slant at one writing is a multifaceted individual, interesting, dimensional, with different sides to his or her personality. Sometimes he wants to be alone to think, read, or meditate (expressed in backhand writing) and at other times he is in the mood for love and people (expressed in the right slant). The person's basic character doesn't change—just his mood or the situation. A reliable, consistent individual may be deadly serious at work but warmly sentimental at home with his family. The slant of his business writing may therefore be coolly upright or slightly to the left. But his intimate personal correspondence may show writing that is inclined ardently to the right.

Take, for example, the following writing. In each sample, the pressure, size, letter formation, and excellent balance between upper, middle, and lower zones are precisely the same. Only the slants differ:

Amendment V: No person shall be field to answer for a capital, or otherwise infamous crir unless on a presentment or indictment of a Grand Jury, except in cases arising in the land or naval forces, or in the Militia, when in actual service in time of War or public danger; nor sha' any person be subject for the same offence to be twice put in jeopardy of life or limb; nor shall be compelled in any criminal case to be a witness against himself, nor be deprived of life, liberty, or property, without due process of law; nor shall private property be taken for public use, without just compensation.

I have another style of writing reserved for family and for persons I have known a very long time. This is also how I might sign a formal document.

Gerry

Both samples were written by a vibrant young housewife–mother who, like many women today, is enjoying two roles—one as housewife and one as serious law student. The variation in slant does not indicate a Jekyll and Hyde personality; on the contrary, it is evidence of an energetic, well-balanced, multifaceted woman.

Don't make the mistake of asking "How can graphology be a reliable pen-picture of the Real Me if I write differently at different times?" Your slant may vary—accidentally or on purpose—but other revealing clues do not change, and a pen portrait is the sum of many parts.

7.

Is Your Lover an Optimistic Cheerer-Upper or a Sourpuss?

What You Can Tell from the Baselines

A pessimist is a man who thinks all women are bad. An optimist is one who hopes they are.
—*Chauncey M. Depew*

An optimist sees an opportunity in every calamity; a pessimist sees a calamity in every opportunity.
—*Anon*

A pessimist is someone who happens to live with an optimist.
—*Anon*

A pessimist is an optimist who endeavored to practice what he preached.
—*Anon*

An optimist is a person who looks forward to marriage. A pessimist is a married optimist.
—*Anon*

Be sure the handwriting specimens you analyze are on unlined paper because the writer's natural baselines will tell you whether he or she's a happychondriac or a hypochondriac.

If you have any trouble determining whether the baselines slope upward, downward, up-and-down, or are perfectly straight, turn the page upside down. If you're still in doubt, fold the paper in the middle with right and left edges in perfect alignment (then the slope is more apparent).

It's best to have various samples written at different times so you will not be misled by a temporary mood caused by fatigue, euphoria, or specific misfortune or good fortune. Conclusions should be based on the *usual* tendencies of the writer's baselines in scripts written at different times.

46

Sincere regards

You don't have to be a professional handwriting analyst to guess that lines that dance exuberantly uphill reveal gaiety and optimism, whereas drooping, falling-down lines mean the opposite. Graphologist Nadya Olyanova aptly compares baselines with the branches of a tree. She says that the up-reaching ones that joyfully embrace the air and stretch toward the sky suggest ecstasy, in contrast to the sadness and dejection of the drooping weeping willow.

For happy love choose the optimist whose baselines swing upward. This person can inspire you with good cheer no matter what adversity you must face together. A positive thinker like the following uphill writer can lift you up when you feel down. No one and nothing can dampen his enthusiasm!

The location will be handy for me as the bus stops right at my door. I will take some of Nan's work down to put on display. It will be a place that I can invite people to visit while the other place was

If the baseline goes up in steps, the writer is a hedonist who lives to have a good time. He may not be the most substantial of lovers, because if you're too sick to go to that party he'll simply go without you. He wants to look on the bright side and be the "good guy," but he can't always live up to this image. No matter how often he's yanked back to reality and even disappointment, he'll keep on trying. You might call him a repeater-optimist!

When the natural baseline of the writing is perfectly straight (no lined paper—that's cheating!), this person isn't easily shaken up, no matter what happens. He's almost always able to control his moods, which are never too optimistic or too pessimistic. He has great stability, which isn't challenged by each little happening. Clear, easy-to-read writing in a straight line reflects a mind that's as carefully calculating as a computer. You can count on this guy for honesty, perseverance, and getting a job done well.

Two of the oldest principles of graphology are "a level line means a level head" and "the straighter the line, the more honest and sincere the writer."

These principles describe the handwriting of the American who became such a symbol of veracity and integrity that he was called "Honest Abe." Lincoln always wrote on unlined paper without a ruler, but his baselines were as straight as if they rested on a line.

The following piece of Lincolnia was recently discovered and fed to a computer for graphological analysis. The IBM 360 in the Handwriting Computer Center in Springfield issued a ten-page report on Lincoln's character, including several points with which all graphologists would agree.

It mentioned the trust*wor*thiness and honesty (as indicated by the straight baselines and frankly open a's and o's). It also said: "You have the drive of a bulldozer plowing through impossible obstacles," "The key to your personality is pride," "You work at being highly respected," and "You conform to the letter."

What about the writer whose baselines descend depressingly? He sees *only* the dark clouds, never the silver linings. With other corroborating negative signs (like weak t-bars and light pressure) he may have a neurotic need to fail or, a morbid tendency toward misery. He could be chronically depressed and refuse to take a chance on new ideas. Perhaps he's lazy and finds excuses *not* to do things. Just as the uphill writer is ambitious and enthusiastic, he's often the opposite.

If your own lines dance uphill and your t-bars are high and strong, beware this gloomy gus. He could throw a wet blanket over all your hopes and dreams!

Sharp, angular writing that slopes downhill is even worse. This person is such an incurable pessimist that you can't change him, cheer him up, or have any fun with him.

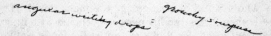

An abrupt drop at the end of the line in a heavy, blotchy script indicates the morbid depression and inhibition of a wretched person who brings misery to himself and others. This sign appears often in the writing of Hitler and Napoleon.

Concave baselines that begin to descend, then curve upward indicate that the writer is at first doubtful, hesitant, or bored with a project. But he strives to overcome difficulties, eventually rallies, and comes to a flying finish!

Convex baselines that begin to ascend, then curve downward at the end, mean the opposite. This person starts out all

afire, then loses his enthusiasm and peters out. No matter how
optimistic he seems, he'll lose interest if he doesn't get im-
mediate results. What a disappointing trait in a lover who
builds you up with a thrilling "rush" job, then lets you down
with a bang. You'll be happier with the uphill or concave-lined
writer.

you are my friend, I didn't know
it then.

A wavy baseline does not necessarily mean dishonesty. It
may if there are other signs, which we'll discuss later on (like
open breaks at the bottoms of a's and o's). Without ac-
companying negative signs an uneven baseline means that the
writer is moody and that his emotions and attitudes may
change with the wind. Although this person may be hard to
know and understand, he can be exciting and will take you on
an emotional rollercoaster.

rollercoaster baselines = versatile, changeable
weathervane sensuality

With sharp, clear, original letters the wavy baseline can
mean versatility and genius. This is a brilliant, creative personality who's bored by routine and too much detail. He just
can't be bothered because his mind is occupied with dramatic
and important ideas. He'll like variety in his foods, activities,
and entertainment.

Remember, it's important to have more than one handwriting sample, or you may mistake a passing mood for the
writer's natural disposition.

The following example was written by a genuine optimist—a
happily married wife-mother-writer whose friends trust her to
cheer them up. She doesn't even despair when a script she's
worked hard on is rejected, but keeps plugging away, rework-
ing and writing new material, feeling that success will surely
come.

Biology: Create life. Estimate the differences in subsequent human culture in this form of life had developed 500 million years earlier, with special attention to its probable effect on the English Parliamentary System. Prove your thesis.

Why, then, the droopy baselines? This was written directly after she had prepared and served a huge Thanksgiving dinner to a large group of family and friends—and she was exhausted! But if you'd only had this sample to go on, you might have mistakenly interpreted the downhill baselines as indications of depression or despondency.

If you learn to get the messages whispered by baselines, you may be able to avoid lovers' quarrels, rifts in friendship, conflicts between co-workers or teammates, and generation gaps. Most of the troubles in these areas are caused by differences in outlook and temperament. Only when we are aware of other people's dispositions and moods can we know how to react to and respect those that differ from our own.

8.
Is Your Lover a Good Guy or a Grouch?

What You Can Tell from the Shape of the Writing

Be amiable if you would be loved.

> —Ovid

Amiable people . . . radiate so much sunshine that they are reflected in all appreciative hearts.

> —Madame Deluzy

There is more of good nature than good sense at the bottom of most marriages.

> —H. D. Thoreau

Those who complain most are most to be complained of.

> —Matthew Henry

The weathercock on the church spire, though made of iron, would soon be broken by the storm-wind if it did not understand the noble art of turning to every wind.

> —Heine

Once it was fashionable to classify people into Dr. Sheldon's three categories: endomorphs, ectomorphs, and mesomorphs. Endomorphs were jolly, genial fat people who were lazy. Ectomorphs were skinny, angular, mentally sharp but sour and dour (like Caesar's Cassius who had "a lean and hungry look"). Mesomorphs were the in-between-fat-and-thin—the athletic hero types.

Judging a person's disposition by his physical build wasn't as reliable as knowing his temperament by the shape of his handwriting. If you want to know how easy or hard someone is to get along with, study the shape of his letters and connecting strokes. Are they round, angular, or garlanded? An ultracongenial, cooperative, easygoing person writes a rounded script; a shrewd, inflexible, "I-want-my-own-way" grouch has a sharp, angular script; a sophisticated charmer scribbles eye-pleasing garlands.

Of course there are good and bad aspects of each, so let's go into detail, starting with the rounded script.

If roundness is the most prominent and consistent feature of the writing, with all m's and n's scalloped like perfect arches, this person is gentle, kind, submissive—perhaps too much so because he has a childlike simplicity that makes him gullible.

An excessively rounded writing with no sharp points to relieve the roundness indicates lethargy and laziness, both physical and mental.

round writing = easy-going, docile, wants peace at any price

Large, round writing, as in the sample below, indicates a desire for independence and admiration that cannot be fulfilled because of the writer's lack of drive and leadership.

My favorite mystery story of all time is;
Agatha Christie's
"The Murder of Roger Akroyd"

A small, round script belongs to someone who is cooperative and gentle and who has great powers of concentration, an inquiring mind, and a talent for detail work.

We're both sorry that we have been missing your classes, but due to Roger's work schedule it is impossible for us to attend.

Medium-sized writing that is so rounded that it seems child-like is a clue to gullibility and immaturity. This person will trust anyone and anything. But his puppy-dog admiration may eventually get on your nerves.

the Rolling Stones.

If sharp, angular capitals appear in an otherwise round script, the person puts up a powerful front—a facade of aggressiveness that is not a real part of his personality.

In most people the tendency is for the rounded writing of childhood to sharpen as the youngster grows up, develops individuality, and matures. The more he thinks for himself, the more pointed his writing becomes.

In Erich Segal's *Love Story*, Jenny Cavelleri's script is described as small and pointed, appropriate for a girl from a minority group who, through concentration, hard work, and aggressiveness, carves herself a place of importance in a snobbish WASP society. But you can be sure that as her love for and marriage to Oliver Barrett IV mellowed her sharp, suspicious nature, her writing became less pointed and more rounded.

Just as excessive roundness suggests feminine softness, an angular script indicates masculine firmness—especially if accompanied by heavy pressure. A clear, angular script that is sharp but easy to read reveals a sharp, critical, fact-loving mind. This person is usually more interested in ideas and things than in people. He's hard to please and you can't put anything over on him or influence him against his will, so don't try! He usually has mechanical or constructive ability and so is mighty handy to have around the house.

An angular writing = firm, strict, aggressive, critical, strict tends to be a Non-conformist

A large, angular writing is your tip-off to an ultra-aggressive personality. This guy wants to be boss and will not play second fiddle to anyone. If you're a women's libber, you'll definitely want to steer clear of him! Many actors and

actresses have handwritings similar to this, particularly those
who have a strong need to be in the spotlight.

*Hope everything is going
great for you!
We miss you!*

A small, easy-to-read, angular script reveals a keen mind.
Here's an intellectual, good at detail and analysis, usually a
specialist in his field. He has a few, well-chosen friends, so
if you're among them count yourself lucky. He shows good
judgment in handling money.

Success often comes to him who strives.

*small, clear angular writing =
keen mind. A good detail man
and analyst. smart in money matters*

*small, squeezed-together angular writing = nervous
about money, standoffish, penny-pinching, selfish.*

A well-balanced mixture of rounded and angular letters
indicates an individualist who can nevertheless be amenable.
He's nobody's fool. He won't push you around but won't let
you push him around either. He can be firm or pliable,
depending on the circumstances, and can fit in with different
types of people.

In choosing a partner, look for versatility in the shape of the
writing. If the letters and connecting strokes are *all* angular,
without any graceful curves, you won't get lots of loving from
this iceberg (especially if the slant is leftward or vertical). On
the other hand, if the writing is monotonously rounded,
without any sharp points or angles, this person is a lovebug all
right, but may be as ever-loving to others as to you! Try to tie
up with someone whose script has refreshing and suspenseful
variety: rounded, angular, with occasional sharp, pointed letters.

Annabel Lee.

By Edgar A. Poe.

It was many and many a year ago,
      In a kingdom by the sea,
That a maiden there lived whom you may know
      By the name of Annabel Lee : —
And this maiden she lived with no other thought
      Than to love and be loved by me.

If you want a lover and/or friend who is popular, charming, and delightful to be with, look for writing formation that is garland-shaped, with m's and n's looking like w's and u's. Here's a good mixer who loves luxury, is poised, suave, cultured, sophisticated, and hospitable, with a knack for entertaining and for making things run smoothly. The fact that he enjoys elegant surroundings doesn't mean he's lazy or wants to be one of the "idle rich." Many garland writers are very industrious, but they usually manage to have glamour jobs entailing much socializing and aesthetic environments.

I feel that our permissive society will eventually threaten the very security of our country. Misunderstanding and lack of knowledge of basic fundamental objectives of other nations toward the U.S. by the people of the U.S. is appalling!

If both rounded *and* garlanded m's and n's appear in the same script (each is the reverse of the other), this is a sure sign that the writer is very easy to get along with and delightful company. If you're the jealous type, you might want to think twice about getting involved with this person: you may end up having to share all his or her charm with others!

If your potential lover writes a light-pressured, garland-shaped hand with weak t-bars, be forewarned: he or she is *so* responsive and *so* agreeable that he can be taken advantage of. A real patsy or pushover can be identified by low, saucerlike garland forms.

Occasionally you'll find a script that's arcade-shaped. Sometimes this occurs in the writing of architects, engineers, designers, or inventors who are involved with "structures." Otherwise it indicates inhibition, lack of spontaneity, artificiality, and affectation. This person is a stickler for convention and wants you to be, too.

He can be uncomfortable to be around, for he may be taciturn, suspicious, skeptical, scrutinizing, and mysterious. Being with him is a bit like being in the presence of royalty and not knowing the protocol or what fork to use.

How come you don't want to see my handwriting?
It's one of a kind. It's called manuscript printing.
There was a lot of controversy about the form of writing we were being taught at that time. (way back when I was a kid in New London, Conn). I really do not know how to master the longhand writing other than what I taught myself. Also, over the years, my manuscript printing is not as exact as it once was. (Now that I think of it, neither am I. (Just a little humor).

I may be(your last invitee
to respond but I bet I'm your
first Thank you note to arrive! Hope
it even makes it to Halloween!
So sorry the date was
"spooked" on our calendar. Indeed
life on the lake is hectic, unpredictable,
filled with meetings & planning sessions
+ 'crosscountry instant trips and
heaven knows what else here

If you're just starting out in a new relationship, it's pretty hard to tell whether your lover is easy or hard to get along with. People are usually on their "best behavior" for a period of time. Then, when the honeymoon's over, the truth comes out! But if you study the shape of the letters and the connecting strokes, you'll make no mistakes.

And don't forget to scrutinize your own handwriting as well. Are you loving? Are you so loving that you're an unexcitingly easy conquest? Are you unloving, shrewd, hard-to-please, sharp and critical? Are you so luxury-loving that you might scare away a person with simple tastes or a low salary? Are you so popular, sociable, and charming that you terrify a love candidate who's more introverted? Are you stilted, affected, artificial, and inscrutable?

Only your handwriting knows for sure!

9.

Is Your Lover an Egotistical Show-Off or a Shrinking Violet?

What You Can Tell from the Size of the Writing

That man who lives for self alone, lives for the meanest mortal known.

—*Joaquin Miller*

Every bird loves to hear himself sing.

—*German saying*

Every man can tout best his own horn.

—*Scottish saying* ("tout" means blow)

Without self-flattery there would be little pleasure in life.

—*French saying*

Self-love is more cunning than the most cunning man in the world.

—*La Rochefoucauld*

Self-love is not so vile a sin as self-neglecting.

—*Shakespeare*: Henry V

In general a person who writes a large hand wants a prominent place in the center of things. He sees things as a whole and cannot be bothered with details. This is the splurgy show-off, the extravagant egoist who will do almost anything to attract and hold attention. Don't choose a mate with excessively large writing unless you want to be dominated and bossed.

Very small writing belongs to the detail man, one who tends to be more of an introvert. This person makes a good accountant or researcher because he doesn't get bored with the nitty-gritty. The small-script writer tends to be more of a thinker, while the large-script writer is more of a doer.

Although these opposites often attract, there may ultimately be trouble in their relationship because the large-script writer likes large gatherings of people, lots of noise, parties, and high living (particularly if the script slants to the right), whereas the tiny, clear-script writer prefers solitude and a few, interesting friends, if any.

Huge writing with conspicuous flourishes indicates a person who craves an audience and must be seen and heard.

Extra Large = Ego, Extravagance
Delusions of Grandeur

A large, right-sloping writing belongs to someone romantic and gregarious, who loves people and conversation. He is not necessarily as egotistical or grandiose as the extra-large-script writer, but he has a robust interest in life and people. Celebrities often write in this large, ambitious, attention-craving hand.

Large = ambition, sociability
Love of People + NEED of approval

If a script is large and graceful, with artistic capitals, the writer loves to be the "life of the party" and usually is.

Mr Dickon
Miss Dickon —

A large, strong writing with heavy t-bars shows that the writer knows what he wants, is determined to get it, and can accomplish many things with amazing versatility and competence. Here powerful emotions are balanced by a firm will.

A large, light writing indicates acute sensitivity. This person also has ambition and the desire to attract attention but isn't forceful, vigorous, and energetic enough to get what he wants. Quite often frustration is the result.

Both my imagination & nose are running away with me so until I run head on into a box of Kleenex this will be all my composition for tonight.

Excessively tall writing is indicative of the person who likes to tower over others—both literally and figuratively.

Very small writing indicates conscientiousness, concentration, and modesty. This writer is usually an individualist, an intellectual who doesn't worry about what others think of him. He sees the world as infinite, his role as modest, but he wants to do a good job of whatever he is assigned. Napoleon wrote a large, heavy hand; Ghandi's script was tiny and weak, but his influence was just as great, if not greater, and certainly longer-lasting.

You seemed tired or sad . . . . . . or "something" at class tonite (and maybe a little of the same at the class before)

If it's something in your personal world, I can only wish you "God fix it" but if it's because you're disturbed with our

Here's the writing of a successful author, one of the top favorites in the slick magazines:

> My mother has told me
> of your enthusiasm for my
> stories, and of course I'm
> pleased to know of it.
>
> I want you to know my
> mother has nothing but good
> words about your class --

One of the most brilliant inventors this world has ever known wrote a tiny, clearly readable script with original formations and a combination of logic and intuition (connections and also breaks between letters):

> In the year 1887, the idea occurred to me that it was possible to devise
> an instrument which should do for the eye what the phonograph does
> for the ear, and that by a combination of the two all motion and
> sound could be recorded and reproduced simultaneously. This
> idea, the germ of which came from the little toy called the
> Zoetrope, and the work of Muybridge, Marié, and others has
> now been accomplished, so that every change of facial expression
> can be recorded and reproduced life size. The Kinetoscope is
> only a small model illustrating the present stage of progress
> but with each succeeding month new possibilities are brought

into view. I believe that in coming years by my own work and that of Dickson, Muybridge Marié and others who will doubtlessly enter the field that grand opera can be given at the Metropolitan Opera House at New York without any material change from the original, and with artists and musicians long since dead.

The following article which gives an able and reliable account of this invention has my entire endorsation. The authors are peculiarly well qualified for their task from a literary standpoint and the exceptional opportunities which Mr Dickson has had in the fruition of the work.

Thomas A Edison

In choosing a lover, you are probably best off with the medium-script writer. This person is well balanced emotionally and intellectually. He or she is not too reserved or too outgoing, too self-effacing or too egotistical, and is a good compromise between a thinker and a doer. As a lover, he wears well, is adaptable and easy to understand and get along with (especially if the letters are gracefully rounded and there's regularity in other aspects of the script).

Winston Churchill said that he had never persevered in anything as he had in trying to convey his thoughts and feelings forcefully and easily, convincingly and persuasively to his fellow men.

My profound thanks to you

Another thing to look out for is size variation. If the size changes constantly, the writer is sensitive and unreliable, with mercurial moods that can have you climbing right up the wall!

If the words taper from large to small, this person starts to tell everything but then clams up before the conversation gets too intimate. He or she is an eloquent speaker but not terribly frank.

Writing that trails off to a mere line indicates diplomacy. This person can be a glib speaker but one who reveals nothing. He's usually successful in politics!

On the other hand, writing that gets larger belongs to the person who can't keep a secret. Often he's too frank and talkative, especially if the a's, o's, and d's are open at the top.

Compare your own handwriting's size with that of your lover. Are they similar? Quite different? If the latter is the case, read Chapter 13, "How Opposite Should You and Your Lover Be?" It can make a difference in how you'll get along!

10.

Is Your Lover a Spendthrift or a Saver?

What You Can Tell from the Margins

You can give without loving but you cannot love without giving.

—*Bowden*

Whoever allows his day to pass by without practicing generosity and enjoying life's pleasures is like a blacksmith's bellows—he breathes but does not live.

—*Sanskrit Saying*

If you always give you will always have.

—*Chinese Saying*

Since so many lovers' quarrels are caused by money, it's important that you know your lover's reaction to economic matters before the two of you get involved. If you have a couple of writing samples, the margins should tell you all you need to know.

As a rule, neat, even margins around a clear script indicate culture, breeding, and good taste, whereas narrow margins indicate a more economical nature (perhaps imposed by poorer circumstances). You can check out this difference in the writings of the wealthy, cultured gentlemen's gentleman George Washington and the self-made, hard-working Abraham Lincoln.

> Upon this boy's faith-
> fully serving out his enlist
> ment in the Naval service
> he is pardoned for any de-
> sertion from the army here-
> tofore committed.
>
> A. Lincoln
>
> Feb. 18. 1865

The following writing is that of a girl with an appreciation for art and beautiful surroundings. Note the exceptionally wide margins:

> Hi!
> Since you didn't
> make it to my house, I
> brought the pills to you.
> Also here's the hand-
> writing sample of my friend.
> Does it tell you anything?
> Love—
> Marge

This writer leaves no margins. He is practical rather than aesthetic, and doesn't spend money on nonessentials no matter how beautiful they are.

The left-hand margin usually indicates the writer's relation to other people, whereas the right margin shows his concern for himself. A wider right margin than left shows that he'll think of his own security first no matter how much he's tempted to spend money on other people and causes. Wide right-hand margins indicate reserve and self-consciousness. If there are added indentations and wide spaces in the right-hand margin, there is a need for privacy.

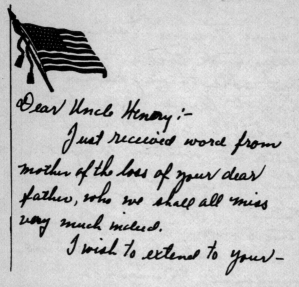

Dear Uncle Henry:—
Just received word from mother of the loss of your dear father, who we shall all miss very much indeed.
I wish to extend to your—

Sloppy margins show poor judgment whether they appear in wide margins (excessive love of beauty) or in narrow margins (bad taste).

What if a writer leaves ample margins, then, after finishing the letter, writes in them? This person is friendly, impulsive, and sociable, bubbling over with *joie de vivre*.

Take, for example, the writing that follows. This lady is a spender, but she spends only on those who need her help. A genuine good Samaritan, she doesn't waste money on frivolous luxuries. Her writing fills not just the whole page but the margins as well. Note also the expansiveness of her writing and the outstretched terminals.

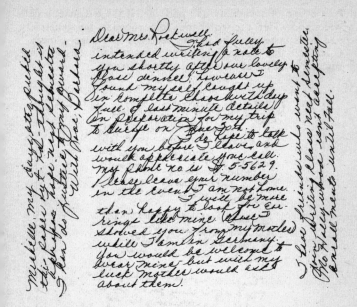

The upper margin (at the top of the page) expresses the writer's respect for the person he's writing to. It is an old custom in Europe for the blank space above the salutation to indicate the status of the recipient of the letter. The higher the position, the larger the upper margin.

We have no such rule in America. But we may unconsciously leave larger margins out of respect for the eyesight of the reader. A large upper margin, therefore, indicates respectfulness—if exaggerated formality.

This is somewhat true also of the lower margin at the bottom of the page, although this is the least important of all four. Usually writing that droops so low as to omit a bottom margin reveals apathy, depression, or laziness. This also reduces the good taste and artistic sense indicated when there are wide, even margins all the way around.

The left margin is the most important and always has been ever since medieval monks held the parchment with the left thumb to keep it from slipping while they illuminated manuscripts. They started the tradition of the wide left margin, although people vary it according to their personalities. A fairly wide left margin shows a love of luxury and fine things.

It is a sign of sociability and partying. If the left margin gets wider and wider, the writer tries to economize, but generosity and good taste win out and he becomes a "budget-blower." Often he's the "poetic" type who saves up for necessities but squanders all for aesthetic pleasures or luxuries.

Less than the coral root, you know,
That is content with the daylight low,
And has no leaves at all of its own:
Whose spotted flowers hang meanly down.

You linger your little hour and are gone,
And still the wood sweeps leafily on;
And you would not have it otherwise
In this one place beneath the skies.

You cannot carry away a flower
From the merest passing whim of the hour,
But there are those that wait afar
To make it tell them what you are.

They choose to forget in the thought of you
The love of the thing you bid them to:
And this is a weariness of the soul,
Which nothing but nature can make whole.

                   Robert Frost

If the left margin is erratic, so is the writer's money sense. He switches from spendtrift to penny pincher!

A too-wide left margin means wastefulness, lavishness, and excessive pride.

Please return your listing of Credit Students in attached envelope. If no credit students, return anyway — noting this fact over your signature — JF

A too-narrow left margin or none at all shows caution with finances. He gets the most for his money and can save.

> *I am writing to explain 'that these rights & particulars in connection with amateur performances do not lie in my mother's hands, at all but in those of messrs Samuel French. My mother asks me to say*

A wide left margin that gets narrower shows that the writer has extravagant tastes but is able to control them.

> *All that I know*
> *Of a certain star*
> *Is, it can throw*
> *(Like the angled spar)*
> *now a dart of red;*
> *now a dart of blue;*
> *till my friends have said*

Another way to test generosity and/or extravagance versus stinginess and/or thrift is to study the spaces between the words and lines.

It is wrong to think that the size of the writing indicates generosity or frugality. A person who writes a large script may be such an expansive show-off that he gives the impression of a big spender. But if there is no space or narrow spaces between words and lines he's expansive and expensive—for you—because he's inclined to order lavishly, then let you pick up the check!

> *Large script with poor spacing—wants to appear generous But is stingy and selfish.*

The small-script writer, on the contrary, may seem so reserved and unobtrusive that he gives the impression of being tight, but if there are large spaces between his words and lines, he's the truly munificent one. He'll probably treat you!

Here's a medium-script writer whose excellent spacing reveals her generous, considerate nature.

I am a 2 + 2 person — in other words — an accountant. A dull business for most but

Remember, don't be deceived by size alone. Spacing between letters is equally important. The following samples belong to a show-off (large script) who spends lavishly to create an impression, and a modest person (small but well spaced) who is truly generous. (Lower loops that swing to the right denote altruism and magnanimity.)

Hope your feeling better! Sincerely

*Thank you so much
for your get well card.
Have just left the hospital.
nurses, doctors, personnel
were simply marvellous.
Hope to see you soon.
For I am and dear you a
wish.
When you are ascending the hill
of happiness, may you never meet
a friend coming down.*

If you are looking for a nice, pleasant lover who is giving but not a spendthrift, look for carefully formed letters, well-spaced words and lines, and full, even margins. It's a general rule that:

1. Wide-open spaces mean an open hand and heart.
2. Narrow or no spacing means tightly closed purse strings.
3. Irregular spacing is a sign of disorganized thinking and action.

You can apply these rules to a person's mental as well as financial attitude. A narrow script with narrow or no spaces between words and lines indicates a narrow mind. This person is overly cautious and is more interested in material things and himself than he is in ideas and other people. Good spacing between words and lines (along with the other signs of affection you have learned) mean the opposite: this person will be open-minded and unselfish—a much more considerate lover.

Always beware of extremes. There are as many problems with a person who's too much of a budget-blower as there are with a too-strict budget-keeper!

11.

What Image Does Your Lover Present to the World?

What You Can Tell from the Signature

Names and natures do often agree.
—*John Clarke*, 1639

A good name is rather to be chosen than great riches.
—*Proverbs XXII:1*

Because a signature is a person's legal identification and usually appears more often than the rest of the writing (especially now in our typewriter-dominated times) it is considered the hallmark of personality and a "symbol of self." Some people make the mistake of thinking that character can be judged from the signature alone. This is not so. Important clues are deduced from the relationship of several lines to each other, margin placement, and many other features that can only appear in several pages of writing.

Still, analysis of the signature can add a great deal to what you learn from the writing samples, if you take certain precautions. First, make sure the signature is authentic. Several politicos use a stamp, and many celebrities have publicity agents sign their names. Second, know the conditions under which the signature was written. Sometimes a person who must sign many papers will abridge, condense, or blur a signature, whereas others may purposely disguise their signature so that it can't be forged.

The relationship of the signature to the regular writing can be one of the most important indications of how the person wants to be seen by others. In most cases, the signature emphasizes the traits the writer wants people to *think* he has. Only when the signature matches the script in zone emphasis, pressure, slant, baselines, shape, size, regularity, and connections is the writer putting his "real" self forward. In this case, his self-evaluation is in synch with his outer personality, and he doesn't have to put on a face for the world.

It's not unusual to find such startling differences between the signature and body of the text that it's hard to believe they were produced by the same individual. A vain, egocentric person may have a bold, flowery handwriting and a tiny signature. He may unconsciously wish to be thought of as modest and shy. On the other hand, a small-script person who's somewhat self-effacing may want to exhibit self-confidence through a bold signature.

If your lover writes a letter the lines of which slope downhill, but the signature slants upward, he may be tired or depressed but he doesn't want to worry you with his "blahs" so he "puts on a happy face" especially for you. This type of writer probably thinks more of your feelings than his own and is a much better friend than the reverse—the uphill writer with the downhill signature. This "poor me" crybaby isn't as bad off as he wants you to think. He's just making a bid for your sympathy instead of being self-reliant.

There can be real danger signals in a downhill signature at the very bottom of the page in which the final stroke cancels out the name. This can be a wish for self-destruction and often appears in suicide notes.

To find out your lover's "sense of self," answer the following questions with regard to his or her signature:

1. Does your lover sign his or her name legibly or illegibly?

This is an indication of whether your lover honestly wants to reveal his or her personality and thoughts clearly or be enigmatic. Illegibility can also denote eccentricity when backed up by other offbeat pen scratches.

2. What about the size?

Is the signature the same size as the body of the letter? If so, the person is natural and aboveboard, the same in public as in private. Consistency in size means sincerity and reliability, especially if there are no flourishes and strange, eccentric strokes.

Sincerely,
Catherine

3. Is the signature the same as the script, both small and clear with original but clearly readable formations?

This indicates a brilliant mind, capable of intense, productive concentration, probably an unpretentious genius.

However its waiting to be defrosted so how about Thurs. May 12th. Sorry to hear you have been so ill. Please come & bring nothing but your pleasant company.
Love
Elaine

4. Is the signature large, matching the big writing?

This is a frankly proud, attention-loving person who probably has acting ability. If the signature is huge with abundant flourishes, the writer is vain, eccentric, ostentatious, and wants to be the center of attention.

Billy

5. Are there strong discrepancies between the signature and the regular script?

If so, this writer probably has a dual nature, presenting one personality to the public that's quite different from his private self.

6. Is the signature disproportionately larger than the text?

This person has a strong need to impress others and be recognized as an important figure. An over-large signature with a small writing means pretentiousness and false pride. Sometimes this is a coverup for feelings of inadequacy.

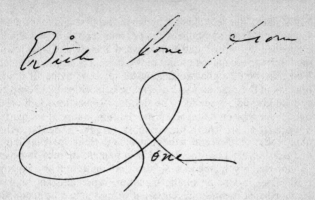

7. Is the signature much smaller in size than the text?

If so, the writer either wants people to think he's more modest than he really is, or else he underestimates himself. The latter is true if the capitals (especially capital "I") are very small.

Very truly yours,

John H. Falk, M.D.

8. Is the signature vertical or left-slanted whereas the script leans toward the right?

This means that the writer may be cool and undemonstrative in public but sincerely warm and affectionate when he's with you. If this is the case, he probably won't want you to be an erupting volcano in front of others, but he may accept aggressive behavior when you're alone together.

9. Do the slant, size, and pressure vary?

This weathervane can't stick to decisions, may be confused about sex, and will be unpredictably different on different occasions.

Sincerely yours,

William S. Clark

10. What is the relationship between the first and last name?

The first name symbolizes the personal ego, whereas the last expresses the writer's attitude toward society and also toward his family (or acquired family in the case of a married woman). You may find a signature that states just one name. If it's the first, as in the case of some self-made celebrities like Napoleon and Rembrandt, it seems to be saying, "Look, I made it on my own!" As women's lib gained momentum, many of its married devotees wrote their first names larger to declare their independence. Several others dropped their married names and used either their maiden or first names, thereby implying, "I am not my husband's shadow or chattel. I am my own self!" The last name of the signature represents the writer's social ego. It is either accentuated or minimized in proportion to his or her attitude toward himself, his family, and society in general.

If the first and last names are equal in size, shape, and slant, there is harmony between self and society and an amicable family relationship. If the first name is conspicuously more prominent, the writer has less esteem for family and society than for himself. In a married woman's signature this may even indicate dissatisfaction with her marriage, her husband, or her in-laws. If, on the other hand, the last name is much larger, the reverse is true. Not only is this person extremely proud of his or her family (natural or married) but he or she may be snobbish and look down on others. In most cases, the family name and/or social position give him or her more prestige and clout than he or she could have achieved on his or her own.

If the first and last name slant differently, there is an inner conflict between personal and family life and between individual and social goals. In a married woman's signature, it may mean that she wants to go out and work, but her husband wants her to stay home. Trouble may be brewing.

11. Where does the signature appear on the page?

The normally accepted place is near the right-hand bottom corner. If this is where your lover signs his name, he is a socially adaptable and (with corroborating signs) conventional person.

If, on the other hand, your lover signs his or her name far to the left, he or she wants to withdraw from society or at least leave his present environment. A left-placed signature that's written backhand in a small, crowded script indicates a fear of the future. This person prefers to live in the past.

A signature that rushes too far to the right—almost off the page and into the margin—means that the person is impatient.

His enthusiasm may fascinate you, but he wastes energy spinning his wheels.

Suppose the signature is all you have, and you want to learn something about the person. Here are some clues it will give you:

Ascending = ambitious, optimistic, cheerful, will work hard to succeed.

Descending = discouraged, depressed, tired (may be ill).

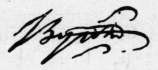

Ascending in steps = constant struggle against depression, fun-loving.

First and last name connected = constructive and organizational ability. Makes full use of his time and potential.

Threadlike connections = has psychic powers and keen psychological insight into other people. He can anticipate public reaction and trends and also has a great ability to solve problems.

Right-slanted = extroverted with a healthy attitude about sex and social relationships.

Left-slanted = sexually shy. You may have to bring him or her out.

Vertical = sexually inhibited. A lover who must think before he acts. It's up to you to get things going.

Extremely original = creative. May be artistic, literary, musical, or scientific genius.

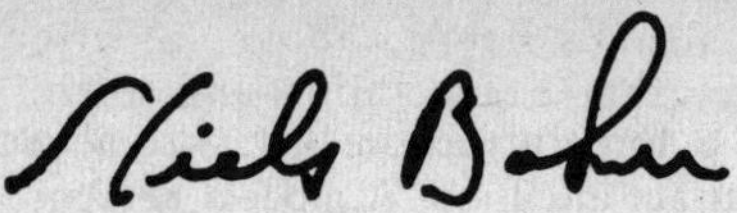

Niels Bohr [signature]

Letters dwindle toward the end of the signature = tactful but shrewd.

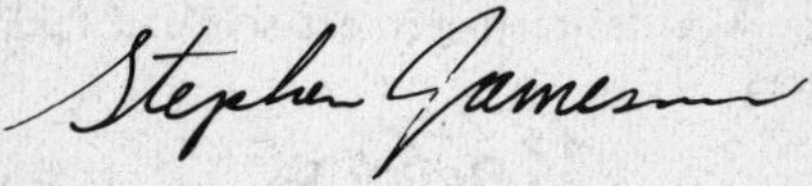

Stephen Jameson [signature]

Letters get larger at the end of the signature = blunt, tactlessly outspoken (especially if the oval letters are open at the top).

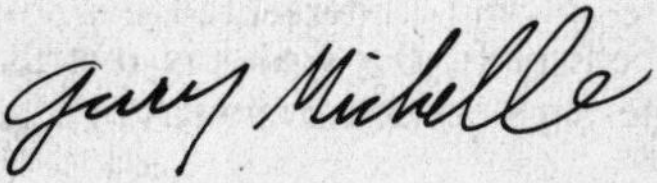

Gary Mitchell [signature]

Muddy, blurred, heavy strokes = sadistic, perverted. BEWARE.

[handwritten note: "There's a new floor wax called"] [signature]

Narrowly squeezed letters = wants his or her own way in sex and can't be easily swayed.

[handwritten: "rely yours,"] [signature]

Superfluous strokes below, above, or after the signature—these represent exaggeration and overdramatization and can mean a forceful personality, magnetism, tenacity, or a desire to attract attention. A modest person, who doesn't do things for effect and who doesn't want the limelight, writes a clear signature without ornamentation.

Underscoring = "Look at me!", assertive ego.

Overscoring = a desire to protect self and family, or just plain selfishness.

If the signature is both underscored *and* overscored (and perhaps overembellished), the writer is distrustful of others, egocentric, and perhaps eccentric enough to scare your friends away.

A circle around the signature means the person wants privacy and protection from the world. He may feel disliked and persecuted and therefore builds fences or walls around himself. This extra curving around the signature is similar to the way you'd put your hands and arms over your head and face if attacked or if an earthquake loosened the ceiling above you.

A period appearing anywhere in a signature (before, after, or in the middle) is another proof of caution and suspicion. *Before* the signature it may mean the person hesitates before starting something like a relationship. If a period appears *after* a mild, passive signature, it means caution, suspicion, and fear. *After* an aggressive signature it means rebellion and defiance. A period *within* the signature shows inhibition and anxiety. It's going to be up to you to bring this lover out. He or she is no self-starter, but with enough other corroborating signs it may be worth your efforts in the long run.

What can you tell from the signatures of the following celebrities?

Marie Curie

G. Urbain

J. Edgar Hoover

John F. Kennedy

Sincerely.

Ed Kennedy
Edward M. Kennedy

Henry Wells

Wm. G. Fargo

Louella O. Parsons

Louella O Parsons

A signature alone won't tell you everything. But if it's all you've got, it's better than nothing. Look for a consistent slant and size, some sharp-pointed letters, and perhaps some witty, original touches. Particularly important is consistency; for no amount of surface charisma or good looks can compensate for the lack of strength, courage, and dependability.

12.
How Does Your Lover Address the Envelope?

As the personally addressed envelope goes out into the world it broadcasts messages about its writer.

How can this be true when we have said that no accurate character analysis can be made on the basis of less than two full pages of writing along with the signature?

How important can the few brief lines of address on an envelope be?

Very important!

Why?

Because the envelope has a special function. No matter how private or personal the letter inside may be, the address *outside* is quite a public matter. It is meant *to be seen*. How it is written therefore expresses the writer's attitude toward other people. Does he or she care as much about others as himself? Does he or she strive to establish open lines of communication or is he secretive and withdrawn? Does he or she want others to admire him or doesn't he care?

The script on the face of the envelope puts its writer on stage, in a public performance for all to see. Condensed as it is in a small space, it offers a mini-study of the handwriting legibility, formation, position, and capitals, and can therefore tell a great deal about the personality of the writer.

Legibility

A clearly written name and address denotes cooperation with the laws of the land and a wish to be understood. If your lover addresses envelopes legibly and his or her baselines are ruler-straight and the a's and o's are open at the top, he is honest and trustworthy. If the slant and pressure are firm and even, you can always count on him or her to be faithful and consistent—not necessarily exciting (unless other unique signs point this way) but dependable.

If, on the other hand, the envelope writing is undecipherable, he or she doesn't give a hang about what people think of him or her. This person is a law unto himself, although he may put on a different facade when trying to win you.

Illegibility along with indications of selfishness, vanity, or rebellion tell you that the writer is so egocentric that no one else's opinions or feelings matter. If unreadability combines with signs of extreme genius, intellect, or originality, the writer may be more wrapped up in his work than in social amenities—but his work may be of greater benefit to mankind in the long run.

Don't be hasty in condemning the writer who scrawls an illegible address. Perhaps the envelope was addressed in a jerkily moving vehicle or under extreme pressure (that's why you should have several samples). It may indicate illness, infirmity, or psychosis (if substantiated by these signs). But under proper circumstances, an illegible address means lack of consideration for others (especially workers) or deliberate secretiveness or deceit (maybe the writer doesn't know how to spell or is ignorant in some way and doesn't want you to know it).

> *Alicia Van Such*
> *9930 Alden ave*
> *Northridge, California*
> *U.S.A*

Numbers

How does your lover write numbers on the envelope?

Clearly formed medium-sized digits mean that the writer is practical about money matters.

> *Mr. F. R. Van Such*
> *% Hollywood Adult School*
> *1521 N. Highland Ave*
> *California 90028*

Oversized numbers indicate an exaggerated concern with money or the things it can buy. Swiss psychologist-graphologist Max Pulver detected an interesting ambivalence in the person who wrote numbers larger than the rest of the script: naiveté and financial impracticality plus a greedy Midas personality. These traits sound contradictory, but both reveal an unrealistic approach to the exchange value of money and material things.

F. A. Rockwell
c/o Pierce College
6201 wininutka
Woodland Hills, Calif.
91364

Small, clear numbers on the envelope are characteristic of individuals who could be mathematical experts. They'd make excellent accountants, mathematicians, math teachers, engineers, or scientists.

Mr F. A. Rockwell Instructor,
Writing For Publication
c/o Reseda Community Adult School,
18230 Kittridge St.,
Reseda, California 91335

If your lover's numbers are ill-formed, smudgy, or indecipherable, don't loan him or her money or trust him or her

to do your income taxes. Nor should this person be encouraged
to seek a job in which mathematical ability counts.

Mr. F. A. Rockwell
c/o Pierce College
6201 Winnetka Ave.
Woodland Hills
Calif. 91364

Even worse than clumsy numbers are those that are touched
up with strokes upon strokes. This usually means neurotic anxiety caused by financial problems.

Thecia Von Such
9930 Aldea Ave.
Northridge
Calif.

13.

How Opposite Should You and Your Lover Be?

Marriages are best of dissimilar material.

—*Theodore Parker*

Opposition is the very spur of love.

—*Smollett*

Nature is upheld by antagonism—passions, resistance, danger are educators.

—*Emerson*

Where there is much light, the shadow is deep.

—*Goethe*

Contrast increases the splendor of beauty, but it disturbs its influence; it adds to its attractiveness but diminishes its power.

—*John Ruskin*

The poets and philosophers give us mixed advice. Some say opposite unions are the best kind, providing excitement and stimulation. Some believe that though the flame is initially brighter, it dies quickly. Which are we to believe?

Well, statistics show that no matter what we have to say about it, opposites do, indeed, attract. Bigots marry liberal humanity-lovers; logical eggheads marry impulsive birdbrains; proud independents end up with cringing doormats; shy introverts with loud, exhibitionistic extroverts; maternal or paternal types wind up with children-haters; energetic athletic people are saddled with sedentary slowpokes . . . and so on. It is also true that marriages between contrasting types of personalities often end in tragedy for one or both partners.

Still, with all the possibilities for disaster, many of us are continually attracted to our "opposite." Why? Because to spend our lives with someone identical to ourselves would be boring. In addition, the duplication of faults and weaknesses (along with virtues and strengths) could be far, far worse than the clash of opposite traits.

On the other hand, if two people are open to change and compromise, character variations can be both stimulating and fulfilling. Both partners must be able to face up to important truths about themselves, each other, and the partnership. When handwritings indicate that you and your potential lover are "opposites," look for *love*, *humor*, and *adaptability* in both scripts in order to avoid later disillusionment. In addition, the comparison should reveal *some* areas of similar interest to counterbalance strong differences.

Let's take a look at a few areas in which opposition may be extremely difficult, if not impossible, to overcome.

Can a humanitarian find happiness with a bigot?

You may answer "yes" if you are thinking of the TV sitcom *All in the Family*. Bigoted Archie Bunker and his people-loving, broad-minded wife, Edith, do seem to get along, in spite of their differences. The reason for their harmony seems to be her forgiving spirit and protective attitude toward her stubborn husband. Edith is able to overlook Archie's faults in an almost superhuman way. Maybe you could be like Edith—but maybe you couldn't.

In any case, fiction is not life and a sitcom gets laughs through exaggeration, witty lines, and character conflicts.

Reality is a *different* matter. A sour bigot can destroy a broad-minded person's cheerfulness and trustfulness. He or she can also cut off valued friendships that don't fit into his idea of "the right people."

On the other hand, someone whose affections are too all-embracing can irritate a partner who considers himself "discriminating." If their home is constantly filled with people, their budget strained by a steady flow of freeloaders, conflicts will undoubtedly arise.

How can this be avoided?

How can you spot this potential source of friction before a harmonious partnership is threatened?

How can you find indications of such irreconcilable differences in your own and your lover's handwriting?

Easy. Just take your clues from the words themselves:

> Narrow—small in width as compared to length; limited in outlook; without breadth of view or generosity; prejudiced.

versus:

> Broad—wide; large from side-to-side; spacious; clear; open: as *broad* daylight.
> Broad-minded—tolerant of other people's opinions or behavior; not bigoted.

The writing of a narrow-minded person will have narrow spaces between the letters and words, and words will not end with a wide, horizontal stroke that reaches out like an open hand. These signs are more liable to appear in the script of a generous do-gooder. These opposites will not enjoy life together unless the narrow-writer wants to broaden his outlook or the overexpansive one is willing to try to limit overflowing affection. Neither broad-mindedness nor discrimination is always a bad quality. But extremes of either can be difficult to cope with.

If the broad-writer also writes a round hand with a forward slant, he or she may be incapable of seeing or hearing evil when it's there. This trusting individual can be an easy prey to crooks and villains. (Some criminal lawyers study the handwritings of prospective volunteers for jury duty and choose these ultra-broad-minded people who love everybody—even those who deserve justice, not sympathy.)

But for most people a broad-minded person is easier to live with than a narrow-minded one. As people grow older they tend to become set in their ways. If you're looking for a mate in the mature age bracket and you are broad-minded, you won't be happy with such an inflexible opposite. If this is the case, avoid a person who writes a narrow script with down-flung terminals (stubbornness) and letters that begin below the line (argumentative). If such a writing appears with no margins, be prepared for a skinflint who's as stingy with his emotions as he is with money and material possessions.

Excessive ego and rigidity are additional warnings that a person will never love anyone as much as he loves himself, no matter what he promises you. Notice the towering capital I's in the following writing sample, taken from a love letter. This man's primary love affair is with himself. He can't stand anyone who detracts from his own sense of self-importance. The rigidity of the writing plus unchangingly sharp, pointed letters and slashed i-dots show inability to adjust to children and an irritated dislike of them.

Life without you would be unbearable. I would lie down and die of a broken heart. I want to be the last person in the world to cause you misery, pain, or heartbreak. I want to make you happy,—you and the boys. The three of you can make me the happiest man in the world, if you let me take care of you, and be everything you ever wanted in a man.

Can an ultralogical person get along with one who always operates on intuition and hunch-power, or will a plodding planner annoy and be annoyed by an impulsive, spur-of-the-moment mate or vice versa?

To detect these traits, examine the connections between the letters within words. Many breaks indicate intuition and flashes of insight and inspiration, especially if t-bars and upper loops are high. No breaks in a steadily connected script mean a logical mind.

If the pen is *never* lifted from the paper between letters, *only* between words and maybe not even then, you know that the writer likes to visualize a project as a whole before he begins it. He or she likes to know exactly what is going to happen and doesn't want anything interfering with his train of thought.

Here are samples of writing from a well-matched couple. Both people are extremely logical and live according to a well-planned routine. Each pens a reclining slant that denotes affection and both have angular letters that reveal good minds and down-to-earth interests.

Permission is given, provided you let me in on your analysis of your own writing. Haven't got no black ink except ball pens, and that isn't representative.

I give you permission, as H. says above; that is, first serial rights are hereby

The negative aspects of continual connectedness occur in a large, rounded, unoriginal, monotonous script. This is the writing of a dull person who doesn't like to vary routine. You'd better not rock his or her boat by suggesting too many novel approaches to lovemaking (or other activities).

On the other hand, the disconnected writer, while not the most predictable guy or gal, does have a lively imagination, and can be full of delightful, insightful surprises. Don't expect a logical chain of thought—this person relies on intuition. He may pick a winner at a horse race because of the horse's name rather than the horse's track record. But, as you know, sometimes these hunches pay off!

Separations or breaks between letters in an original handwriting indicate a bright mind that thinks quickly and can offer you unending stimulation. This person also has some psychic ability. In a highly advanced script, the letters are simplified, almost printlike, as if this quick-witted person wanted to eliminate unnecessary penstrokes as well as nonessentials in thought and get right to the point. Continual disconnections along with high t-bars, i-dots, and high upper extensions indicate an inspirational genius.

A mixture of connectedness and separateness between letters promises refreshing versatility and, in an intellectual, original writing, genius! Often in great minds, a flash of inspiration initiates thought or action, but then logic, research, and experimentation take over, translating the idea into a great work of art or invention. (Look again at Edison's script in Chapter 9.)

Disconnected writing does have its negative side. If the writing has wide space breaks between the letters or if the shape of the script is rounded with varying slant, size, and pressure, this person is too illogical for you to get mixed up with. He or she can't follow a single train of thought and, because of failure to comprehend the importance of connections in human relationships, has trouble making friends. If you want a reliable partnership, look elsewhere!

Can an independent person get along with a dependent one?

This is one case in which opposites *can* get along far better than identicals. If both partners are fiercely independent, with inflated egos, sparks will fly and there will almost always be a clash of wills and unpleasant competition for top billing. On the other hand, two dependent, weak mates will never make it in the cold, cruel world. If each of them depends on the other, they're bound to fail, and if they depend completely on someone else (like a father or father-in-law), they'll lose their autonomy as a couple.

It used to be true that men were the breadwinners, solely responsible for support of the wife and family! Today, thanks to the women's liberation movement, sex roles are far less rigid. The misconception that men-are-always-the-stronger-sex and women-always-the-weaker-sex was so long ingrained in our culture that many early critics of women's rights feared that the new female independence would threaten the solid structure of marriage and the family. But as is proved in such studies as *Beyond the Male Myth* (Dr. Anthony Pietropinto and Jacqueline Simenauer) and as is discussed in Chapters 14 and 15, the new equality of the sexes is adding more strength, joy, mutual help, and companionship to the man-woman relationship. This is especially true when the male is secure in his own masculinity and looks upon an intelligent, independent but loving wife as complementing him instead of competing with him.

Today more and more marriage ceremonies omit the phrases "Love, honor and obey" and "Till death do us part," and substitute sentiments of mutual respect. The typical wedding in a metaphysical church quotes Clifford Gessler's relevant poem in which newlyweds pledge to be "each his own master and the two richer, dearer because of it." They agree to "share body and mind and spirit without giving up freedom; love without trying to absorb; be kind yet not smother with kindness; walk together but neither retard the other's pace."

A love relationship is enriched when "the spark of self-hood" is mutually respected. We think of this as a new concept and perhaps it is in formal marriage ceremonies, but wasn't the idea expressed by the English clergyman-writer Sydney Smith 200 years ago when he said: "Marriage resembles a pair of shears, so joined that they cannot be separated; often moving in opposite directions, yet always punishing anyone who comes between them"?

Here are the handwritings of a happily married couple. The wife's writing reveals an independent, brilliant, strong-willed woman, one who would never be content as just a *hausfrau*. The Greek e's, high strong t-bars and i-dots, intuition-breaks and shrewdness-implying pointed letters indicate that she'd never be happy as a confined homemaker. The expansiveness of the script, extended endstrokes, and wide spaces between words indicate warmth and affection, although the backward slant shows that she doesn't wear her heart on her sleeve. She can "play it cool" when necessary and in public, but she has strong opinions and expresses them bluntly and eloquently. In contrast, her husband's small script indicates that he likes to stay out of the limelight. His logical intelligence (pointed word/well connected), cheerfulness, and sense of humor (curvy i-dots and upturned endstrokes) show that he in no way feels threatened by his wife's achievements but is proud of them (she is a successful writer). In this case two distinctly different personalities (as revealed by their handwriting) complement each other well.

> The time has come for
> those of us who are
> driven to create to turn
> our backs on the drinkers
> of our blood, the eaters of
> our flesh, the inhalers of
> our souls.

> Now is the time for all good men to come to the
> aid of their party — and the time for
> all good women to come to the aid of
> their men. How will I fare? I
> know not — for I have a problem.
> I know two women named Frances — both
> delightful and both a little kooky.

In the case of the following couple, the wife is also more
outgoing and people-loving than the shy, introverted, but intelligent husband. He is rather noncommunicative (closed
ovals) and moody (wavy baseline); but his wife's more rounded
script indicates an amiable person, willing and able to smooth
out any trouble spots in the marriage. Her tall capitals show
pride and independence that keep her from being a doormat.
Although there are many differences in the writing styles of
this husband and wife, their equal pressure (energy and passion) and right slants (affection) indicate important similarities
in temperament.

The things I like to do most
with my husband are: playing golf,
playing gin rummy and cuddling—

Lyla made me write this

In the following sample, the wife's dependence is indicated
by the long initial strokes, small light script, and rounded
formations. Her husband is the Rock of Gibraltar in this union:
firm, logical, commanding. The gracefulness of her writing is
feminine and charming, whereas his script is masculine in
force and firmness, revealing self-confidence and independence
(large capital I's and no beginning strokes).

New England, born and bred am I
I feel I cannot escape the hold it
has on me. Living in California for
twenty years has not diminished the longing
to be once again amid my childhood streets,
old and crooked and to smell again the
cool salty sea air

I consider myself a true American as I am proud of my country, my ancestors and family that worked hard, fought for and believed in a nation that has been for freedom for all and hope that this belief is carried on in the years to come – God Bless America

The following couple—a working wife and her house-husband—are alike in some ways and extremely different in others so that their long-lasting marriage is never boring. Both are sociable (right slant); share a love of life (similar pressure); divide their interests between physical, mental, and spiritual (balance between upper, middle, and lower zones); and inspire their friends with their good nature and sparkling wit (smile-shaped i-dots).

There are, however, some differences between them. Whereas she's mentally disciplined and organized, likes to be on-the-go, and would be frustrated by the monotony of house-work, he's casual, easygoing, and less energetic (he has severe back problems which limit his physical activities). She's a logical thinker (all letters are carefully connected), whereas he's more intuitive (breaks between letters)—a good combination in a partnership that's harmonious in so many other ways!

*Roses are red,
violets are blue,
sugar is sweet,
and this is a silly
saying.
Shirley*

*I will see you
tog, morrow
David*

The following couple (both intellectuals) have similar hand-writings which nevertheless reveal important differences. Both husband and wife are outgoing and friendly (she uses more garlands than he, but he has a strong right slant). His versatile i-dots are sometimes extremely witty (curvy), sometimes con-structively critical (carat shaped), rarely irritable (dash). The wife has great literary ability (Greek e) but she doesn't dot her i's, which may mean that she has a poor memory or that she's too occupied with worthwhile projects to remember other details of life. She needs his sharp, shrewd memory and he benefits from her aesthetic nature and intelligent mind.

"Life is a tale told by an idiot
full of sound and fury
signifying nothing."   Shakespeare

                    Elaine

"Compacted into the small region of Palestine
are all the tendencies all the influences for
good and evil that activate modern man."

from— *The Story of Israel* - by Meyer Levin —

The following man and woman are missionaries, both fully alive and in perfect tune with one another. Their upper zones (spiritual and mental) are high-reaching and equal in size with the lower loops (physical) and the middle-zone letters (practicality). Their mutual love of mankind is evident in the right slant, and their energy and love of cultural sensory pleasures (art, music, and nature) are manifested in the heavy pressure. The husband's ultrareligious nature (the H's reach up to heaven like church spires) is tempered by the wife's modest amiability (rounded letters in a smaller writing). She has great powers of concentration and the literary ability to write a book about their dramatic experiences surviving the horrors of war and confinement with their new baby in a rough prison camp. Their writings point to the reasons why they endured: strong spiritual faith, moral character, vigor, and love for all humanity as well as for each other.

"Go, labor on; 'tis not for naught,
Thy earthly loss is heavenly gain:
Men heed thee, love thee, praise thee not;
The Master praises - who are men?"
                    Ruth J. Clingen

"God sent not His Son into the world to condemn the world but that the world thru Him might be saved"

Herbert H. Clingen

This next husband and wife have handwritings that reveal strikingly similar personalities. Yet these two are never bored by one another. Can you see why? Perhaps it is because they both have brilliant minds (small, clear, sharp scripts) and similar controlled emotions and temperaments (vertical slants). Although the husband evidences more self-confidence than his wife (slightly larger capitals and firmer pressure) and is moodier (varying slant), they have basically similar, logical viewpoints, can appreciate humor (smile-shaped i-dots), and share a high level of intelligence. Both are PhD's—she a mathematician, he an executive engineer.

Look to this day,
For it is life, the very life of life.
In its brief course lies all
The realities and verities of existence.

Look to this day
For it is life, the very life of life.
In its brief course lies all
The realities and verities of existence.

The husband is the boss in the following marriage, as you can tell from his firmer pressure, higher capitals, strong long t-bars, and pointed letters. The wife is more patient, affable (rounded m's and n's), and cheerful (upturning endstrokes). They both are extremely intelligent (small, clearly formed script), affectionate (same right slant), and share an interest in sports and other physical activities (extended lower loops).

> I'm standing in a window and the lighted object moves in my direction. I know that they know I am there. I also know that they want me to know they are there. I'm filled with a reverential fear. I don't think that I wake up at that point but I never remember anything else occurring.

> You! You're the one that caused things like graphology, astrology, palm reading and Psychological Stress Evaluation to become sciences. If you could have just straight out told me what you are like when I asked you personal questions instead of telling me.

These cases demonstrate that opposite traits in your lover can indeed mean compatibility and a long, healthy relationship—*if* there are enough similar traits to balance them. It's no easy matter to find the ideal complement to your nature. The right blend of opposite traits and sympathetic alignment doesn't just come along every day. But, with your new knowledge of graphology, if and when it does come your way, you should be able to recognize it. Then, once you've settled on your choice, nurture the relationship and watch it grow!

14.
For Women

Being a woman is a terribly difficult task since it consists
principally in dealing with men.

—*Joseph Conrad*

It is not true that woman was made from man's rib. She
was really made from his funny bone.

—*Sir James M. Barrie*

It is strange what a man may do and a woman yet think
him an angel.

—*William M. Thackeray*

Three women were asked the following question: suppose
you were shipwrecked, and you and a man were washed
ashore on a desert island. Just the two of you. What kind of
man would you want him to be? One woman replied, "I'd
prefer a superbrain who could teach me things and never be a
bore." The second disagreed. "Not me! I'd rather he'd be a
macho guy who knows how to love, hunt and fish and clean
and cook whatever he catches." When they turned to the third
girl, she said with emphasis, "I'd settle for a good obstetri-
cian."

If you're like the first girl and prefer brain over brawn, you
wouldn't mind being isolated with a man who writes
something like this:

*The breadth and depth of a company technical
expertise can be counted to bear in support of
a Naval Activity at a local facility. This cadre
will accomplish fast response task assignments.
Where time permits expertise residing elsewhere
within the company will also be used.*

He's a superbrain and could probably teach you lots of intellectual things, but *you'd* have to teach *him* how to unlock
his inhibitions in order to let himself be a good lover. Oh, yes,
he's capable of loving you (after all, you're the only female
around) but only after much deliberation, so you'd better be
more mentally than physically hungry. But once he's made up

his mind, watch out! The small, precise, concentrated script that denotes cold aloofness may be an icecap on a churning volcano! What a challenge for you to convert his sexual fantasies (shown in the incompleted but wider lower loops) into tingling realities!

The second girl would be happier with the man who writes like this:

> *I have tried to please her but it seems that all this is improving is my typing.*

He's not nearly as mentally complicated or as inhibited as the first man. His right-slanted, passionate writing and heavy pressure show him to be the physical type and, best of all, his o's are closed enough to guarantee that he won't tell all her secrets when they're back in civilization. The long, rhythmic lower loops promise a fulfilling sex life as well as practical know-how in dealing with physical needs and problems. The rising baseline reveals optimism and cheerfulness and the curvy i-dots indicate a marvelous sense of humor. His happy-go-lucky nature and quick quips will keep her from loneliness and boredom.

The following third example of writing may fulfill the practical request of the third girl. He's an M.D.—brilliant, cool-headed, experienced, and knows what he's doing at all times.

> *Self made men believe in Their creator.*

> *To thine own self be true, and I must follow as the night the day, thou canst not be false to any man.* ———

You might try this fantasy game out on yourself. It's not a bad idea to select your lover according to how he'd stand the test of isolation with you as his sole companion. Nor is it that far removed from real life. When you hitch your wagon or, more importantly, your *self*, time, energies, reputation—in fact your *whole life* to one mate—your relationship can at times be as cut off as if you *were* on some remote island. So go ahead and fantasize: get in touch with your own needs and desires. Then, when you have a pretty fair idea of your choice for a life partner, let graphology help you find him.

First, you need a plan of action. What will it be? Before the women's lib movement, a popular actress shared her success F's for making a man say "yes."

Find him
Fascinate him
Flatter him
Fuss over him
Fondle him

If none of these works, then:

Forget him

Let's look at the first F. *Find him*. In order to find the guy who's Mr. Right for you, you must know the honest truth about your own character. Are you passive, aggressive, easy-going or irritable, intellectual, athletic or inactive, introverted, fun-loving or serious?

Do you think you'll be happy with a man whose interests and temperament are similar to yours or excitingly different? Do you want everything peaceful and lovey-dovey at all times or do you like a good fight once in a while?

According to psychoanalyst Dr. Theodore Rubin, a dominating, strong-willed woman may enjoy a dependent, adoring male whom she can mother or prefer an even stronger-willed man who will master her (like the old-fashioned patriarchal heads-of-families in *Life with Father* and *Cheaper by the Dozen*).

Are you finicky clean or creatively messy? Career-minded or domestically inclined? Flexible or rigid? Mental, physical, or both?

How educated are you? How educated do you want your lover to be? A girl who's a brilliant, cultured PhD might enjoy dancing with a handsome, well-dressed high school dropout but couldn't stand him as a steady diet. Most women want to look up to a man intellectually, or at least be on equal footing. Therefore, you're probably heading for disaster if you choose a lover who's your mental inferior, no matter how strong the sexual attraction between you!

Are you chronically late or unable to make a decision? Many men won't tolerate a woman who procrastinates. (You can spot this in your own writing as pre-placed t-bars and i-dots and a slow, pokey script.)

A man hates to be kept waiting, whether a woman's late for a date or stalls over an important decision. *He* may have taken ages to decide that he wants to make your affair permanent and legal. But when he tells you of his verdict, he doesn't want you to keep him dangling. Think about it, yes, by all means. But don't spend so much time looking that you don't ever leap!

Actress Marsha Mason and comedy-playwright Neil Simon married less than a month after they met when she starred in his play *The Good Doctor*. Even though he was mourning the death of his wife of twenty years and Marsha had never entered into any relationship that quickly, she says:

> I have some advice for young people today. If you're in love, you can sit around and think about it until you've thought yourself out of love. Or you can just move on it quickly like we did. Why not? From the minute I met Neil, I felt like he was someone I'd known all my life.

Are you a perfectionist? Constructive criticism of your mate is okay, but most men despise carping, destructive criticism of the "Why-can't-you-do-anything-right?" variety (tent-shaped i-dots in a sharp, pointed script). Maybe yours is the kind of man who will value your ability to help him see and correct his faults, but maybe he isn't. If the stems of the t's and d's in his writing are looped, he's sensitive, so tread lightly. If you love him a lot and he has many more good than bad points, it may be better to overlook his flaws altogether.

What other qualities do men dislike in women? In a recent national magazine poll an equal number of men and women answered the question "What qualities do you least favor in the opposite sex?" The qualities *men* favored *least* were: hostility, possessiveness, jealousy, bitchiness, lack of stability, excessiveness, under-assertiveness (the doormat) or over-assertiveness (the battle-axe), extravagance or stinginess, gossip, no sense of humor, procrastination, vanity, phoniness or presumptuousness (pretending to know more than they do), sloppiness, loudness, vulgarity, nagging, apathy, belligerence; too much makeup, *immaturity*, *dishonesty* (playing games), and *cruel vindictiveness* (toward men or anyone else).

The women's response? According to the survey, the qualities *women* admired *least* were a macho attitude, dislike of women and their causes, inattentiveness, a superiority complex, stupidity, weakness, impatience, irresponsibility, inflexibility, prejudice, laziness, grouchiness, insensitivity, dirtiness, *immaturity*, *dishonesty*, and *brutality*.

These three last traits—immaturity, dishonesty, and brutality—appear on both the men's and women's list as qualities least admired in the opposite sex. Do you agree? Could you spot these undesirable qualities right away, or would you have to know your mate a long time before they came to the surface? Each of them is easily detected in your potential lover's handwriting (as well as your own). Let's see how.

Immaturity

A Babydoll female or a Peter Pan male may be charming and fun for a while but an alliance with either of them would have the sticky-sweet impermanence of cotton candy. Immaturity is the single biggest cause of marital misery and divorce according to Dr. Paul Poponoe, founder of the Institute of Family Relations.

Watch for signs of immaturity in your script as well as your potential lover's. If you use an ultra-rounded, large copybook style with the long beginning strokes of childlike dependency, do your best to grow up. If the man you're attracted to writes with such signs of immaturity, tell him to get lost before he ruins your life or turns you into a slave or a mother.

Marriage has been called "Our last and best chance to grow up," but it doesn't work instant miracles. Both partners must bring to it a certain degree of unselfishness and a sincere desire to become mature.

Exactly what is immaturity? It's the inability to go on with life's music. Like a stubbornly stuck phonograph needle, a person's behavior is likewise stuck in one of the five phases of character development:

Stage 1. The infant is totally self-concerned; he's indifferent to the feelings of others who exist only to fill his needs.

Stage 2. The child expands love to parents, especially to the one who can do more for him than anyone else.

Stage 3. In a few years the child goes outside the home and makes friends, usually with youngsters of his own sex.

Stage 4. Adolescents show increased interest in the opposite sex in a general way.

Stage 5. The interest in the opposite sex grows deeper and usually focuses on one person. If there is real maturity, the concern will be unselfish, the person showing as much concern for the loved one as for himself or herself.

At which stage of development are you? A person's chronologic age isn't as important as these way stations along the road to total man-woman love and fulfillment.

Neither calendar age nor sex determines maturity. But maturity determines better relationships with your man and also with other people!

No matter what age you are right now, you don't need to dread the passing years if you honestly work hard at developing the qualities that give a woman charisma and attractiveness all her life! There is scientific proof of this! Ever since 1928 the Institute of Human Development at the University of California at Berkeley has studied 214 women at different ages in their lives and found that "There is only a negligible relationship between being attractive in early adolescence and being attractive at forty" (according to Dr. Norman Livson, one of the 200 doctors, psychologists, sociologists, and psychiatrists from all over the world who participated in the study). In addition to maturity and consideration for others, the mutual attributes of these ladies who were as desirable at forty as at eighteen were:

cheerfulness
interestingness
liveliness and expressiveness
social perceptiveness
appreciation of sensory sights and sounds
sincere understanding of men
active participation in life

Are there indications of maturity in your handwriting? If not, can you consciously try to develop them in life and also in your script?

No matter how young or old you are now, if you begin to cultivate these "plus" traits, you'll always be attractive to others—even to younger men who prefer such qualities to youthful sex appeal. Most of them agree with John Travolta, Warren Beatty, Charles Bronson, Henry Winkler, and Bruce Jenner.

When these stars were asked what they wanted in a woman, Travolta put maturity absolutely first. He said, "Older women make better companions because of their life experiences. I can talk to them and know they're listening deeply to what I'm saying." Beatty said he goes for "vulnerability, sensitivity, and brains." He wants a woman who's more interested in other people and in what's happening in the world than in herself. Bronson likes refinement, style, class, and breeding (characteristics of maturity). He says, "It's only a lady who can turn an ordinary man into a gentleman." Like the others, Winkler isn't turned on by clinging vines. He prefers a gal who has her own life and purpose. Jenner is annoyed by young women who throw themselves at men. He's glad that older women know better.

Maturity is a constellation of such delightful traits that it produces an enduring charisma that doesn't fade with age.

Here are some handwritings of forty-plus women who can hold their own in charm competition with girls half their age. Can you spot the indications of maturity?

(Cheerful)

(Interesting, intellectual)

(Charming, congeniality)

(Wit, liveliness, and intelligent versatility)

I called Edith R. & told her how much money we had, why I couldn't bear it with someone to give you next week, and how much fun we had buying a dress & stockings at Ohrbach's.

(Optimism, generosity, and sensory awareness)

Sample of
Handwriting
Dickie Dare
saw a Cow
Moo Moo said
the Cow.

(Practical idealist, understands men)

we do and say. When we know that we have not, it brings lean into our souls. Unless we confe this, we harden our hearts and eventually have no conscience to worry us or remind us.

Even in youth-worshiping Hollywood, the First Lady of Costume Design is mature, exceedingly talented Edith Head who has designed for more than 1,000 pictures over a span of thirty-eight years! Her exciting script tells you why. The large, heavy-pressured lettering denotes vigor, sensory awareness, and a magnificent art and drama sense. She loves colors and aesthetic forms. As the sample says: "As a costume designer in motion pictures, I am interested in anything '*visual*,' which of course is why I think handwriting is so important."

Her up-flung t-bars express optimism and ambition in line with her own words: "I've been designing for the 'perfect figure' for years and have learned how to make a woman look ten years younger and ten pounds thinner." The contrasting down-flung endstrokes signify determination and persistence and carat-shaped i in "Edith" and angular m's and n's attest to a shrewd, critical nature. You'd better be competent if you want her approval. Some letters connected and others separated show that her fine mind is well balanced between logic and intuition.

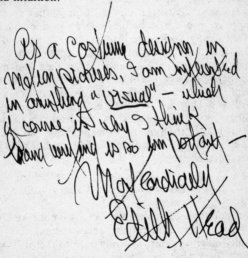

Dishonesty

How can you detect dishonesty in a man's (or woman's) handwriting? Not by one sign alone. Dishonesty is complex and may differ in degree, from the little white lie to major thievery or infidelity.

If your lover's handwriting is regular and clearly legible (regardless of its size, slant, or pressure), he's probably open and aboveboard, with no deep, dark secrets. It also helps if his baselines are perfectly straight, and his oval letters are uncomplex, unlooped, and sometimes open. If his a's and o's are consistently wide open, he may talk your ears off, but at least he'll be frank and honest. If he does have faults or even shady dealings in his past, he'll probably yak enough to eventually tip you off.

So much for indications of honesty.

What are the signs of dishonesty?

There are several danger signals, four or more of which should appear in a script before you cross a man off as a crook. That's why you should never judge a person on the basis of a few lines of scribble or a signature alone. Also remember that everyone has faults (even thee and me) and many can be corrected. For instance, someone who omits or writes faint, weak t-bars in a light-pressured script may have a weak will and thus be led astray, but perhaps with understanding, love, and firmness you can lead him in the right direction (if you're the type of woman who's into "causes," saving souls, or happy in a maternal relationship with a man, as some women are).

Ten Clues of Dishonesty, Deceit, and Hyprocrisy

(If four or more appear in a man's scrawl do not take him for a lover or let him snare you into any relationship.)

1. Totally illegible letters and numbers so that they seem to be different from what they should represent. (He's *definitely* hiding something.)
2. Smeared, smudgy writing that has been retouched and crossed out.
3. Ink-filled loops and ovals.
4. A snakelike baseline (never straight).

5. a's and o's open at the bottom.

6. Double or triple loops *within* such letters as a's, o's, and d's.

7. Tangled words and lines—a messy, confused script. (After all, isn't dishonesty moral confusion?)

8. Many unnatural breaks within letters. (Breaks and open spaces between words are okay, as they denote intuition, but if *letters* are split, watch out!)

9. Sneaky-looking connecting strokes and terminals.

10. Weirdly distorted lower loops (along with some of the above signals).

Remember that there should be several of the above in one writing and they should outnumber the favorable traits before you give this man the gate! But if there aren't enough good qualities (good looks and a smooth line don't count) to counterbalance the bad, and four or more of these recur—get *rid* of him pronto! Better still, don't get involved with him in the first place.

Brutality

Brutality is another red light that should signal you to stop before your life is ruined. It's impossible to find happiness or fulfillment with a sadist unless you're a sick masochist. In that case you need treatment as much as he does!

According to Dr. Elissa P. Benedek, Clinical Associate Professor of Psychiatry at the University of Michigan Medical Center, 50 percent of American wives are physically abused. Although their reasons for putting up with it, their fates, and their physical degrees of suffering may differ, they usually have one thing in common: each insists that the brute was "wonderful" before she teamed up with him. The "I-had-no-idea" syndrome keeps recurring in the outrageous cases that are discovered, which is a small percentage of the millions of such tragedies that take place. (Women suffer beatings in silence even more than they do rape, which occurs at least ten times as often as statistics show.)

But you *can* predict a man's brutality by studying his inner nature as revealed in his handwriting, and by trying to find out everything you can about his psycho-history, childhood, and family life before you met him.

Signs of brutality in a script include blotchy, muddy, unclear writing, blots and filled-in letters, weirdly heavy pressure, irritation streaked i-dots and heavy t-bars, depressed lines, or other signs of disturbance or frustration.

In addition to the frequency of those clues, you should carefully study the *absence* of gentleness, generosity, and unselfishness.

You may also be spared the agony of living with a wife-beater if you look into the findings of Dr. Robert Whitehurst, Professor of Sociology at the University of Windsor, Ontario, Canada. In his recent studies, he lists eight forewarnings of trouble.

1. His family has problems of alcoholism, drugs, divorce.
2. His father or older brothers are violent.
3. He has a drug or drinking problem.
4. He's the kind who hates to feel trapped (and looks this way at marriage).
5. He's promiscuous and unfaithful (the guilt trip caused by cheating can make a man mean).
6. He hates women . . . perhaps he's had bad experiences with them and must fight back.
7. He hates his job . . . or is underpaid, unappreciated, or harassed, or may even be unemployed.
8. He's hypercritical of his wife and blames her for all his woes.

If you've been truly honest in your self-evaluation, you should have a pretty good idea of your own faults, weaknesses, and negative traits. You should also know how to recognize some of the worst qualities—those major destroyers of happiness—in your potential lovers.

Now, how about that second F in a plan of action: Find him, Fascinate him, Flatter him, Feed him, Fuss over him, Fondle him. *Fascinate* him. Now that you know the qualities men admire *least*, how do you go about cultivating the qualities men admire *most*? If you are not now enjoying a satisfactory relationship with the opposite sex, is it because you are unconsciously frightening them off? Turning them off? Failing to turn them on?

Psychoanalyst Dr. Theodore I. Rubin has worked out a system of L.Q. (Lovability Quotient) ratings to tell you (in his opinion), "what makes a woman lovable."

According to his vast experience with men and women in love and marriage, he says that to achieve a high L.Q. evaluation, a woman must understand the little-boy characteristics that stay with a man throughout adulthood. If she has younger brothers and has observed their younger years of development she knows how much the male needs the approval and rewards that come from "Big Momma," so she's willing to play this role of praising him and bolstering his ego. She's not enigmatic or sullen about what's on her mind but expresses her emotions frankly and is always ready to forgive and forget. She never adds to his frustrations but initiates love behavior and subtly teaches him how to give her utmost pleasure in their lovemaking. She doesn't flirt with other men or try to up-stage her man when they are out in public. On the contrary, she's his best audience. She also takes pride in herself and her own achievements. "Her natural lovability—uncluttered by overwhelming self-concern—develops along with her self-esteem and self-growth. To the extent that a woman finds herself lovable, so will others." So says Dr. Rubin.

The first complete study of male sexuality since the Kinsey Report (which came out in 1948) conducted by Dr. Anthony Pietropinto and Jacqueline Simenauer and called *Beyond the Male Myth*, proves that women's lib didn't just emancipate women *from* men but also *for* men! The confidential questioning of over 4,000 American males showed that the average one much prefers the independent, intelligent girl to the docile doormat of yesterday. He also wants an emotional attachment to accompany the physical attraction that draws members of the opposite sex together.

Surprisingly, sexiness comes *sixth* on the men's list of desirable qualities in women—after concern for his needs, sincerity, affection, intelligence, and self-confidence. Other admirable traits include a sense of humor, good health, fidelity, imagination and agility, tenderness and variety, and "warm-blooded aggression."

Too many women make the mistake of *under*estimating men by *over*estimating their response to physical attractiveness rather than more enduring character attributes. When psychologist Dr. Anne Steinman asked over 500 women to describe every man's ideal woman, their answers coincided with the old-fashioned concept of "beautiful-but-dumb-and-docile." But when the same question was put to 500 young men, their answers rated intelligence, alertness, and cheerfulness right up there with beauty. Furthermore, their preferences in pulchritude didn't mean perfection of features, but neatness, naturalness, and charm.

In other words, the winning traits are ones that can be detected in the mirror of handwriting (which reflects *real*

character) rather than in the mirror on the wall (which reflects
only outward appearance).

A report by Dr. Joyce Brothers, based on the responses of
leading psychiatrists, gives the following list of traits men
desire most in women. Let's take them one at a time and see
how each is reflected in a woman's handwriting. Then look for
these vital signs in your own script!

*1. Sexual generosity and a refusal to give love as a reward
or withhold or limit it as a punishment.* Handwriting shows
consistent ardor in long, lower loops in an uncramped,
free-flowing script.

> Dear Mrs. Rockwell,
>   In the few weeks since I've
> been coming to your Monday night
> Class, I've felt informed and
> reinspired toward writing. I look
> forward with excitement to your
> lectures and your enthusiastic
> interest in your students.

*2. Another shoulder for the wheel and the willingness to
help bear the financial responsibilities.* Look for clear, regular
writing with various formations of the same letters and a mixture of angular and rounded shapes to the script.

> We just finished sorting through a
> three-months accumulation of 4th class
> mail. Let me tell you — there's no

*3. A loyal opposition which offers him frank, constructive
criticism within the framework of her loving and appreciating
him.* Occasionally open ovals and some tent-shaped i-dots in a

round or garland script that doesn't show the rapier-points of
sarcasm or too-sharp angles.

*Group's Structure block,
Don't be!*

*Your advice has a
way of bouncing about in
one's head until it finally
makes the difference in
our writing.*

4. *Ability to win friends.* Graceful garland connections between letters and words. Some intuition breaks within words.

Came too highly recommended.

*For what inconvenience I have
caused you, my regrets.*

5. *Emotional independence.* No long, dependent beginning
strokes to words but a clear, direct start with the initial letter.
Slant not too inclined to the right—the letters may even stand
up straight with a vertical regularity. The pressure is not too
light or the t-bars too weak and short. Proud, tall, printlike
capitals.

*are making a trip
into the past— (or some
thing similar) - a trip*

6. *Capacity for love.* At least some of the writing slants to
the right (unless she is left-handed or has purposely cultivated
a backhand script). Even then there should be pleasing
rounded curves, extended terminal strokes instead of those
that curve backward or hook sharply. (A preponderance of

these are telltale signs of selfishness, jealousy, possessiveness, and acquisitiveness.)

a road last week thinking I would call and say "Hey — time for a visit" Didn't do it though because I've been on a diet all week to lose five pounds.

Dr. Joyce Brothers and the psychiatrists questioned feel that the happiest love relationships are those in which the partners cherish each other without smothering, share interests without interfering, and constructively criticize and guide without carping and blaming. Her favorite definition of love is Harry Stack Sullivan's idea that it is "the ability to show the same tenderness and concern for another person as you do for yourself."

It's up to you to enhance your own life through a mutually happy love relationship. No matter how independent, educated, and into her "own thing" today's woman is, she's still the most important bulwark of a man-woman partnership.

A millionaire bisexual rock idol who has everything money can buy and all the fame and adulation anyone could dream of says, "I'm looking for a lasting, meaningful relationship, preferably with a woman *because a woman will work harder to make it work!"*

15.
For Men

Give me a woman's handwriting and I will tell you her character.

—*Shakespeare*

In the old days, men rode chargers. Now they marry them.

—*Philip Wylie*

There is no worse evil than a bad woman and nothing has ever been produced better than a good one.

—*Euripides*

Read the following statements. If you find yourself agreeing with any of them, it's clear that you've been having some difficulty finding who is Ms. Right for you.

> Men have many faults
> Women, only two:
> Everything they say
> and everything they do.

There's no music when a woman is in the concert.
Women at best are bad.

—*Thomas Dekker*

Women are demons that make us enter Hell through the doors of Paradise.

—*John Dryden*

Woman is the very root of wickedness, the cause of the bitterest pain and a mine of suffering.

—*Tulsi Das*

In *Cymbeline* Shakespeare wrote, "Who is't can read a woman?" The answer of course is he who learns insight through graphology. You won't be able to tell by a woman's physical appearance or by the vibes she sends reverberating within you. But you can tell a woman's character by looking into her writing.

Of course, to find the perfect date or mate for you, you must really know the truth about your own character. Analyze your own writing to know your vices and virtues, your disposition, interests, and needs, before looking for someone to fulfill them.

Where, for example, would you stand in the study of male sexuality conducted by Dr. Anthony Pietropinto and Jacqueline Simenauer and reported in their book *Beyond the Male Myth*? Their research proves that sex isn't the be-all and end-all for *all* men. Of over 4,000 men polled, only 19.8 percent rated sex as their greatest joy in life; 61.2 percent enjoyed sex but didn't consider it life's most important pleasure; 11.4 percent expressed the opinion that most women feel: that its greatest significance is in expressing love; 4.2 percent liked sex as a physical release without psychological or spiritual meaning or commitments; 1.7 percent rated it of less significance than business, sports, or hobbies. Only 1.4 percent said sex wasn't important at all and 0.7 percent felt that sex was obligatory and something that was expected of them.

In which group would you fit? How would you like your lover to feel? Even though sex is the glue that holds some relationships together, there actually are some couples who have a low sex drive but have so many other things in common that they get along just fine. If you choose a woman whose attitude about sex is similar to your own, you stand a better chance of having a long and healthy partnership.

When two partners write with equal-length lower loops and similar pressure and slant, they usually enjoy a harmonious sexual relationship.

What about your stand on women's rights? In order to predict how you'll get along with a new woman in your life, face the facts about your preferences and prejudices and discuss them openly with her. For instance, would you want your wife to work and supplement your income so that the two of you could afford to travel? Would you be happy as a house-husband who stayed at home with the children every day while your spouse went off to her executive-level job? Such issues will undoubtedly affect your love affair or marriage. Only by knowing exactly what you want and what your lover wants can you avoid unsettling events later on.

Before you find yourself trapped into the role of either woman-hater or womanizer try to learn the true character of a girl. How can you do this accurately enough so that you won't get too involved with a girl you think you can't live without, only to learn too late that she's someone you can't live *with*? How can you know ahead of time whether her sparkling champagne humor will go flat or bubble annoyingly when you're in trouble? Will she be a gold digger, penny pincher, or brilliant budgeter? A frigid iceberg or overpowering volcano? A builder-upper or tearer-downer? Argumentative or amiable? A bossy career girl or housewife-mother-homelover? Is she gullible? Skeptical? Loyal? Fickle? Possessive? Jealous? Zealous? Discreet? Indiscreet? Vain? Sarcastic? A thinker, drinker, or stinker?

Judging character from appearance is so popular that it has many names: body divination, body language, people-reading, or "somatomancy" from the Greek words for "body" and "prophecy." Can all these various kinds of characterology help you know what a woman's really like? Let's consider Dr. Sheldon's classification of people into three types: endomorphs (fat people who are easygoing but can be dull), ectomorphs (skinny ones who are mentally sharp but dour), and mesomorphs (the in-between-fat-and-thin who are athletic hero types but conceited). All that this can possibly do for you is to help you tell from a girl's body size if she's ectomorphically built for speed or endomorphically built for comfort—that is, providing she'll surrender at all. It still doesn't indicate whether she will or won't. The unreliability of the Sheldon system is increased when you stop to consider that today's crash diets can temporarily trim a natural endomorph to ectomorphic proportions and fool you altogether.

If you choose a young, svelte girl for a life partner, she might balloon into a fatso later on. That's why many men take a good look at the physique of her parents. If a skinny girl's mama is broad-beamed now, you might tactfully ask to see old family snapshots that go way back. If now-plump Mama was slim in her youth, you have a preview of what daughter will probably look like later on. This genetic factor is one you should consider in ways other than obesity. If you love her enough, resign yourself. If not, look elsewhere.

Naturally you should consider such things as diet and exercise, especially if they are important to you. If you're athletic and you'd like for your mate to share your favorite sports with you, don't get tied up with a lazy, slow-writing girl whose handwriting is extremely rounded and large. But if you prefer to play tennis, golf, or handball with male buddies and want a glowing fire, bed, and a bedmate waiting for you after a game, she might make you happier than the kinetic, "oh-darling-take-me-with-you-I-like-sports-as-much-as-you-do" type.

You can't really tell if a woman's right for you by other physical features, although some authorities say ears tell all. Large ears are supposed to indicate temper and pride; long, narrow ears mean she's jealous, whereas tiny ears show a small, vain mind. Other character experts say you can tell a girl's personality by studying her hands. If she has square fingers she's practical and orderly. Tapering fingers mean she's sensitive and artistic; long fingers show patience; short ones, impulsiveness and a craving for action; thick fingers mean she loves luxury, whereas thin fingers belong to the fretful worriers. If her thumb is large and set low on her hand, she's intelligent and determined; if it's widely spaced from her hand, she's generous and independent; but if she frequently hides her thumb in a half-closed palm, she's shy, inhibited, and probably won't be a very exciting date. But if there are little pads at the base of the thumb and on the finger-tops, she's sensuous and passionate.

Many doctors and psychiatrists consider graphology more dependable than physical or psychological tests, which tend to make the testee nervously aware of being examined, often defeating the purpose of the investigation. But when a person doesn't have to face Rorschach ink blots and psychological gimmicks, when he merely writes, his mind is on *what* he's writing instead of the formation of the script. So, according to many psychiatrists, including Dr. Hector J. Ritoy, no means of personality probing is as quick and reliable as graphology, especially if the patient is put at ease so that he writes naturally without self-consciousness.

That's the secret! The unconsciousness of the writing. So, when you get a girl's handwriting in order to analyze it, be subtle. Don't blurt out: "Show me your writing so I can tell if you're a swinger." Find an excuse to write her a letter that she'll have to answer in writing. If you have more than one candidate for your affection, so much the better! Write all of them letters that'll make them write back to you, whole letters complete with signatures.

When you know what kind of woman you're after, look for indications of the attributes you consider important in her writing. Do you want a woman who's warm and friendly?

Look for the right-sloping slant. Passionate? Find the graceful, long-looped f's, g's, y's, j's, and p's. Agreeable to your whims? Rounded m's and n's. Gracious and sociable? A garland-shaped script. Energetic and athletic? Heavy pressure and rhythmic loops. Enthusiastic? Long t-bars. Generous? Extended endstrokes. Cheerful? Uphill-marching baselines and up-curved endstrokes. Versatile and original? Clever, unique, and varied ways of writing the same letters. A keen sense of humor? Wavy strokes and curvy t-bars and smile-shaped i-dots.

If a palpitating passion flower is what you want, you'll steer clear of the girl who writes an inhibited, natural backhand with light pressure and towering upper loops (while the lower loops are short or missing), whose a's and o's are closed, and who writes with unrelieved angularity and sharp-pointed tops of letters (especially s).

If all of her letters are connected without breaks between them, she's so logical that you'll need an intellectual line to break down her resistance. But if there are frequent breaks between the letters, she's basically intuitive and impulsive and you can plan your strategy accordingly! Tapering letters mean that she's tactful and diplomatic and may be putting you off in a sugar-coated way, but if her letters get larger at the end of each word (and her a's and o's are open), she's tactless, can't keep a secret, and is apt to antagonize people with her frankness. She may hurt you at first with her blunt refusal, but look for the other signs that she *will* eventually give in, like heavy pressure, rightward slant, and long, lower loops, and don't take "No!" for an answer!

Once you've decided she's the woman for you—and she agrees—learn more and more graphology to learn more and more about her hidden character. Every pen-scratch will tell you more about her than many years of being together. For instance, look what different formations of the single letter t reveal:

X She likes fun and romance and is flirtatious.

t She's talkative and sensitive—handle her with velvet gloves.

t She procrastinates, always putting off till tomorrow what she should do now. She'll keep you waiting.

t She's impulsive, enthusiastic, adventurous, always on the go.

t She'll indulge in physical pleasures, has a sense of humor.

t She's self-controlled and inhibited and doesn't give in to temptation.

t She's ambitious, likes to be the leader.

t She's repressed, doesn't have or exert much energy.

t She lacks confidence. If she always eliminates t-crosses she can't concentrate and has a poor memory.

t Low t-cross shows she has little imagination.

t Medium high t-crosses show she's practical and dignified.

t The higher the t-bar, the more imagination and adventure she has.

t She's cheerful, ambitious. She has high goals and optimism about reaching them.

t She's domineering, determined. She'll have her own way or else!

t She's tenacious and persevering . . . won't give up and will call the shots.

t She's sensitive and probably lacks initiative.

t She's extremely touchy. All triangles in a writing mean extreme sensitivity.

t If t-bar gets heavier, she's slow to anger but WOW, when she's mad, look out!

t   T-bar heavy at first, then light—she gets her dander up but gets over it quickly, without holding a grudge. Her eyes may shoot sparks and she may be prettier (more fascinating) when angry. But don't tempt fate!

t   A looped t-bar indicates extreme persistence.

t   An in-curved t-bar is a sign of selfishness and jealousy.

If the t-bar connects with the next word, the writer has great constructive ability (whether it's mental or physical depends on other indications in the script).

While you're working hard to find your ideal woman, remember she's also out there choosing you—and just as carefully! What kind of traits is she looking for?

According to psychologist Dr. Theodore I. Rubin, a man with a high "Love Quotient" is one who is interested in and involved with his wife and children, regarding them as his full partners and allies. He wants to be a "student lover" all his life and is eager to know about his woman's moods, feelings, and needs. He knows how to express his love to her as well as how to communicate all his emotions, including anger, fear, frustration, and other negative feelings. As he expects her to be able to forgive and forget, so can he. He regards his wife as a mature adult and doesn't keep important problems or financial affairs from her. He appreciates the way she functions as wife, mother, and/or in a career, and tells her so. He is not a mama's boy, nor does he let loyalties to his previous family come before his devotion to his wife. He doesn't discuss their marital problems with anyone else.

The man with the high L.Q. rating likes and respects women—especially the one he chose to marry. He takes good care of himself for her so that he'll be around to see their children grow up. He does whatever he can to contribute love and harmony to the home atmosphere so that the children will grow and thrive—and become lovable too!

That's one expert's viewpoint on the ingredients that may help you build a happy love relationship and, hopefully, attract the kind of woman who will be a loyal and devoted partner.

And remember, when you're scrutinizing the handwriting of your prospective lover, don't look for perfection. If you *do* happen to find the perfect woman, she'll doubtless be looking for the perfect man and won't want to bother with the likes of you. After all, you wrote that first letter as bait to lure her—and she may be as busy analyzing *your* writing as you are looking for clues in *hers*!

But if you really want her enough, don't give up. Remember Ovid's words: "Whether they give in or refuse, it delights woman to have been asked."

16.
For Teens

The desires of youth show the future virtues of the adult.
—*Cicero*

Live as long as you may, the first twenty years are the
longest half of your life.
—*Robert Southey*

Being young is the test of tension.
—*James Michener*

Do you know what you want in life? Popularity? Fame?
Love? Enough money to be independent? Do you know how
to achieve your goals, or are you trying so hard in the wrong
ways that your efforts are self-defeating, perhaps leading you
in opposite directions?

Are you bogged down by problems like most of America's
18 million teenagers? If so, are your crises unique and specific
or are they the general ones shared by many of your peers?

What are some of the problems faced by today's youth? The
lack of communication between generations seems to be the
primary one. ("No one listens to me . . . nobody cares," etc.)
Other major youth problems according to recent surveys include:

Search for personal identity ("Who am I?")

How to deal with sexuality ("Which way should I go in the
tug-of-war between peer pressure and parent pressure?"
"Everyone's doing it. Why shouldn't I? I don't want to be an
oddball.")

What about work? ("Should I get a job? How? When?
Where? What for?")

Future shock ("Where's my life going and what will the
world be like tomorrow? What about nuclear wars? Runaway
inflation? The rape of the environment?")

Pressures from these and other problems have caused the
alarming rise of teen suicide, alcoholism, drug addiction,
prostitution, and various crimes. Most of these tragedies stem
from wrong-way attempts to solve problems which lead not to
solutions but to worse problems. In many cases there could

have been happy solutions via right-way understanding and self-understanding . . . by looking *inside* a person's character instead of outside for the answers.

Millionaire John Wanamaker was once asked by some scientists to finance their overseas explorations. He pointed to the leader's head and asked, "Why go so far away? The greatest unexplored areas with the richest resources in the world are right here in the human brain."

Many of us are flocking to such movies as *Star Wars*, *Close Encounters of the Third Kind*, *Galactica*, and *Meteor*, and their myriad film and TV imitators. Our government has been spending billions of dollars and manhours to probe *outer* space when *all* of us need to venture more into the unexplored realms of *inner* space. Our very success in space would not be possible if NASA did not zero in on the inner minds and characters of applicants before they are selected to become astronauts or aerospace workers. Even after someone proves that he or she has the courage, calmness, know-how, discipline, alertness, and physical fitness to become an astronaut, he or she must undergo many more tough tests to prove ability for space flight.

Can he follow orders quickly, cheerfully, and efficiently? Will he remain cool and clear-thinking in an emergency or will he be inclined to push the panic button? Will he get along with others in a cramped, uncomfortable situation? Can he endure complete solitude? How will he react to being cooped up in isolation for many hours, days, or weeks? Will his mind stay sharp when it has no external stimulation or communication?

Obviously everyone can't answer "yes" to all such questions or pass the difficult test to prove his or her ability to become an astronaut. Maybe you can't, but maybe there are things you *can* do, such as win a skateboard stunt race or play a Mozart clarinet concerto or build your car's motor from scratch. Maybe you haven't discovered or developed your special supertalents yet, but why hurry? There's lots of time for you to enjoy venturing into different fields to find out what you enjoy doing and can eventually train to do exceptionally well.

It's a mistake to try to be someone or something you're not or to act in a way contrary to your self. Fortunately, the name of today's game is naturalness. Gone are the weird, phony makeup fads that used to make high school campuses look like Halloween parties. One example of "Know thyself . . . be thyself'' is Christina Ellen Moller, America's Junior Miss of 1977. Even though she was taken on a whirlwind tour of our major cities and exciting places, she never changed from her down-to-earth, small-town self nor did she alter her basic values. When she was asked what her "reign" taught her that she didn't know before, she replied: "That I'm not meant for big-city life. I'm from Jonesboro, Arkansas (population 30,-000), and got scared out of my wits at all the crowds and noise. I can't get over the way people dress in big towns. They don't care if a style is a fad; they go right out and buy. At home, we make sure it's here to stay before we invest money."

What are *your* values and character traits? You must know your *real self* with all your limitations and capabilities before you decide on your activities, life work, or love partner. No matter how much you hero-worship another person, don't ever feel that you should try to be like anyone else because your true personality may be basically different. If you do try, you may turn out to be a faded carbon copy instead of the radiant original you could be!

Take, for example, a teenager named Sheri. Her older brother, Carl, and sister, Judy, love parties, games, people, and dramatics. Their parents are screen stars and the whole family acts, tending to make fun of Sheri because she's tongue-tied in large social groups and is too shy to try out for parts in school and church plays. Once when she did, she stammered, stuttered, forgot her lines, and was a total failure. Let's look at their handwriting.

Sheri's actress-mother writes like this:

Dear Alice:
Please telephone me at
your earliest convenience —

Sheri's actor-director father writes this way:

Are you going to tell me at this late date my wife and I should never have?

Sheri's brother and sister write in the same large, ultradramatic, extroverted way, like this:

Mom, Sorry I wont be home for dinner tonite as I

Sheri's dramatically different personality is reflected in her handwriting. No wonder she felt like such an outcast!

I'm just a Nobody in Nowheresville. Everyone else in my family has Talent But I'm a zero!

Sheri is *not* "Just a nobody in Nowheresville." It's true that she is shy, what you would call an introvert (small backhand slant). But she's also highly intelligent and cultured (well-formed letters and garland connections). She has a good imagination (high t-bars); literary and artistic talent (Greek e's); willpower (regularity of script) and marvelous powers of concentration (though small, the writing is clear and readable). She's also logical and yet intuitive (some letters are connected, whereas others are not) and she has a great sense of detail and love of nature.

Sheri can become successful in work that will use these abilities. She's too young to decide on a lifetime career now, but she enjoys studying tiny plants and animals under a microscope and could be a marine biologist who writes and illustrates her own books!

It's impossible to force a chicken to give milk or a cow to lay eggs, so why expect yourself or someone else to do something he can't do when he probably has talents and abilities that would enable him to do his other special thing successfully?

On the other hand, if there are some qualities you'd really like to develop, some faults and vices you'd like to eliminate, *can* you? There are many of us who can benefit from making changes for the better. Are you one of them? If you don't feel good about yourself, can you *really* change so that you will be proud and happy to be you?

Of course you can! Emerson wrote, "Make the most of yourself, for that is all there is of you." So why not do everything possible to get to the root of whatever in your own character is holding you back? Why not be your own shrink and actually transform any frustrations into fulfillment?

You can do it. As strange as it may seem, you can change your personality by changing your writing! This process is called graphotherapy, a term inspired by two French scientists who cured patients by having them change their handwriting: Dr. Pierre Janet and Professor Charles Henry. Later graphotherapist Paul de Sainte Colombe compared writing to starting a car by turning the key in the ignition and stepping on the gas pedal. But the car does not run because of these movements alone. The engine activity is obviously as important. By the same token, the pen won't move across the paper by itself; your brain powers the movements of your pen.

Handwriting is really "frozen movement" because it captures unseen brain action in visible form. Your brain tells your hand and fingers what and how to write, so your pen-scratches are really mind writing. Graphotherapy is a marvelous method of retraining the brain. Instead of the messages flowing from your gray matter to the formation of words on paper, the process works in reverse; the improvements you make in your writing send signals back to your brain, which in turn directs changes in your character.

Suppose, for example, you are hot-tempered, a fault which continually gets you into trouble. This trait shows up in your handwriting in the heavy, clublike, down-slanting t-bars. Graphotherapy teaches you to practice lightening and straightening the t-crosses, at the same time signaling to the brain "Count to ten when you get mad!" Think of others and how they'll react to your hot-headed explosions! After a month of daily and nightly writing-changes programming this message into your brain, you should begin to notice changes in your personality. Soon your temperament will cool down without your having to think about it.

Of course, just changing the writing alone won't work instant magic. You must also try to express your improved personality in action which "speaks louder than words."

Sandra came to me in tears—not sad but angry, indignant tears. After she'd been Jim's steady for over a year he'd asked Marci to go to the big prom instead of her! She thought it was because Marci was petite and pretty and dressed sharply. But I was determined to find out the truth.

After I calmed her down somewhat, I asked if they'd had a fight. She replied, "Sort of. Everyone fights once in a while. We've had bouts before, and it was always fun making up. But there's no making up this time—or ever!" she wailed with fresh outbursts.

When I examined her writing I saw why Jim had turned off. Can you?

Who needs him anyway?
Not me! that's for sure!

Her heavy-pressured, angular-shaped words proved she liked to have her own way, and her down-slanting t-bars showed her domineering nature and bad temper. When I told her this, she denied it hotly—thus proving it! "I do *not* have a temper!" she stormed. "You'd be mad, too, if a boy didn't tell you where he was taking you and you dressed all wrong. He made me feel like a yuk when I wore tattered jeans and a faded T-shirt, expecting burgers at the beach, and we went to a fabulous place. Then when I dressed up, we went to Slimey Slim's. I told him off so he wouldn't do it again!"

He didn't. He didn't call her again, either. So when I suggested graphotherapy, she agreed to change the handwriting clues to her bossy, hot-tempered breakup scene with Jim. She practiced rounding her sharp-pointed letters, writing with less pressure, and crossing her t's less aggressively, reminding herself at the same time to be more feminine, congenial, cooperative, and less tense and hot-tempered.

Part of Sandra's trouble had been lack of communication. Her a's and o's had been so tightly closed and knotted that I guessed she never even asked Jim where they were going. She admitted she hadn't. Now she realizes that talking things over is better than being disappointed and letting inner resentments build up to a temper explosion.

This is the way Sandra used graphotherapy to soften and refine her formerly thick pressure and round out the sharp angles of her writing to more pleasing curves. She also practiced changing her cold, introverted backhand to a more friendly right slant, her down-slanting t-bars to lighter, higher lines, and her tightly closed ovals to frank and open ones.

As her writing became more feminine, so did she!

Everyone needs people that's for sure. And if you're loving and lovable you will be loved.

In addition, I suggested that she start to call herself "Sandy" which sounds more friendly and chummy than the rather formal "Sandra." She agreed and went along with the graphotherapy daily for a month. The new, warm Sandy attracted so many friends of both sexes that she didn't even miss Jim.

By learning to read your true traits in your handwriting—the bad as well as the good—you can practice changing your writing in order to change your character. But before you embark on this thrilling adventure, you must convince yourself of the following:

"I really want to improve my personality."

"I want to know the whole truth, and nothing but."

"I believe I can correct my character faults by seeking clues in my writing and by concentrating on changing them."

"I will *Think Write* and practice positive thinking and positive doing along with positive writing."

"I won't expect instant, overnight miracles. My character wasn't built in a day and it can't be rebuilt quickly either. I will consciously and conscientiously practice applying graphological principles in all my writing—homework, letters, notes, diary—every day."

Once you've made up your mind to try graphotherapy, how do you know what to change in your handwriting in order to produce the desired personality change?

You already know more about graphology than you realize. Suppose, for example, two boys ask you to the prom and the first boy's handwriting slants and stumbles every which way, while the other writes an even, rhythmic script with graceful, gliding lower loops; you know which boy will be a dream on the dance floor and which will be a nightmare! Or suppose you meet two girls:

1-a flashily dressed, loud-talking show-off
2-a modestly garbed, soft-spoken type

Then you're given two handwritings and asked to guess who wrote which:

a-a large, flamboyant, ornate script
b-a small, clear, neatly written sample

Would you have any trouble matching *1* with *a* and *2* with *b*? Of course not!

Couldn't you tell the difference between the script of a cheerful, ambitious pace-setter and that of a pessimistic droop? You don't have to be a genius to tell whose writing leaps uphill and whose lines drag down. Haven't you noticed that your own writing soars upward on happy days, but when you're depressed, your lines nosedive with your spirits? When that happens, *force* yourself to write uphill until you feel as upswinging as your words!

What if you love listening to Elton John but have trouble keeping your mind on your studies? You probably have a large, scrawly script. Make yourself write small, clear letters, and as you keep concentrating on doing this over and over, you'll be improving your general ability to concentrate as well.

Have you ever noticed how much some people look like their handwriting? An egoist writes tall, proud, "Look-at-me!" capitals and signatures; a shy person, small ones. If you love people, you lean toward them with a hand-writing that also inclines to the right. You reach out your hand in welcome, and the endings of your words also extend to the right. On the contrary, if you dislike or fear people, you instinctively turn back to yourself and your own thoughts, and your handwriting will also tend to turn to the left. A self-involved person often writes endstrokes that, instead of reaching outward, curve backward. This type of person is usually so afraid of rejection that he or she rejects others before they can reject her.

Suppose that's your trouble. You're such a hiding-your-light-under-a-bushel, shrinking violet that just reciting in class makes you nervous. If so, your capital letters are probably short, your t-bars weak, and your signature as self-effacing as an apology. Start right now to change your writing. Exaggerate the height of your capitals, strengthen your t-bars and downstrokes, and enlarge your signature. Keep underlining it for increased self-confidence. Remember, an underscore that goes backward and stops there shows a tendency to dwell in the past, whereas if you practice underscoring to the left and back again to the right, you'll develop an onward-and-upward attitude that'll put you ahead of the game. It'll help too if you increase your pressure and strengthen t-crosses and downstrokes in a firm, regular rhythm.

Is your natural writing the small backhand of a bashful introvert—and you really don't want to be one? Start now to reach toward other people by slanting your writing to the right. Extend your terminals, widen your margins and spaces between words and lines. Let yourself go! Add these changes to uphill lines for effervescent enthusiasm, ambition, and optimism. As you concentrate on changing your slant from left to right, think about swinging your thoughts from yourself to others.

But what if your writing already slants far to the right? You know darn well you're sympathetic and affectionate, but still not as popular and appreciated as you'd like to be. Maybe you're *too* affectionate. This can scare people away—especially if you're a girl who's interested in a boy who wants to play it cool and not become involved or "possessed." Furthermore, the boy you want to attract might think your gushiness insincere. In that case, try writing more vertically. The straight up-and-down slant represents self-control and head-rules-heart, and as you consciously remind yourself to straighten your slant, you'll unconsciously train yourself to master your strong emotions.

Now let's look at some specific teenage problem areas and see how graphology can help solve them:

Identity ("Who am I?") If this is your problem, and for

most teens it's a major one, practice enlarging your capital letters (especially I) and underscoring your signature until you have increased your self-confidence so that you feel that you can find special magic in just being you.

Sex ("Which way should I go in the tug-of-war between indulgence and self-restraint? Between peer pressure and parent pressure?") The chapter "How Sexy Is Your Lover?" explained that passion is revealed principally in the lower loops and heavy pressure. But the under-zoned letters also indicate athletic and other physical activities. Therefore, releasing excess energy in sports is a good way to sublimate strong sex urges.

If, on the other hand, you decide to go along with the permissive New Morality and you fall for an ardent person, try to choose one whose handwriting shows the "plus" clues of empathy (rightward slant with regularity of slope and size); high ideals (tall strokes in the upper zones, preferably as high as the lower loops are long), and closed ovals (so your lover won't blab about your relationship). Don't get involved with someone whose script shows the signs of dishonesty discussed in Chapter 14 or a person who writes extra-large, showy capitals (especially I). This egoist will use you as a sex object and never put your feelings on a par with his own.

Work In considering long-term work or a life career, study your temperament and decide what you'll be best suited for. If your writing shows that you're an extrovert, you'll be better off working with people—perhaps in sales, personnel, acting, teaching, or the clergy. But if you're basically an introvert you'd probably do better in engineering, research, editing, accounting, or a lonely job that would drive an extrovert bananas.

When you are happy in a job, or have settled on your life goal (at least for the time being), you'll solve another major problem that teenagers share with people of all ages: how to be loved. Psychiatrist Dr. W. W. Broadbent says that love must be earned and that if you want to be loved you should ask yourself what you're doing to deserve it. Are you doing too little? Too much? The wrong things? Instead of spinning your wheels trying to be interesting, try to be interested. Don't be onstage talking and performing all the time. Put yourself in the audience admiring and applauding others. Don't blame someone else for your faults. Be yourself, and be sure that's a really considerate, compassionate self who cares as much or more for others as for himself. If there are negative signs in your writing, correct them, thus improving your personality so that you will be more loving and therefore more lovable.

Remember, it's a whole lot easier to change when you're young!

17.
Does Bad Writing Mean Bad Character?

Conformity gives comeliness to things.
—*Robert Herrick*

Either do as your neighbors do or move away.
—*Moroccan Proverb*

Most people can't understand how others can blow their
noses differently than they do.
—*Turgenev*

Novelty is the parent of pleasure.
—*Robert Southey*

. . . if Noah's ark had had to be built by a company, they
would not have laid the keel yet . . . What is many men's
business is nobody's business. The greatest things are
accomplished by individuals.
—*Spurgeon*

Commercials tell us that regularity is necessary for good
health, and throughout this book we've observed that
regularity in the slant, size, shape, and pressure of handwriting
indicates consistency of personality and emotional stability.
Does this mean that you should cross off your list of potential
lovers those who write irregularly or illegibly? If everyone
were to do this, our race would probably dwindle and die out,
because ever since most American schools stopped teaching
penmanship there has tended to be more individuality and less
of the conformistic, calligraphic writing of yesterday.

In childhood we were taught to write a round copybook
form. But usually, as a writer develops his or her own individuality, so does the writing. As the child breaks away from or
perhaps rebels against adult domination, corresponding
changes will occur in his or her script.

On the other hand, persons whose writing retains the
roundness and rightward slant of childhood tend to maintain
amiability and compliance as they grow older. If the roundness

is unrelieved and the script rather large, the writer is also gullible and a starry-eyed "follow-the-leader" type. Not for you if you enjoy surprises and are looking for a relationship that's as breathless as a roller-coaster ride!

If you're a nonconformist who craves excitement and variety in your life, you may want a lover who's as "way-out" as you are. In that case, search for a handwriting which, like the following, is full of contradictions and uniqueness, and a challenge to decipher! Is the sixth word "dashing," "startling," "darling," or ??? Would you recognize the word "conclusions" if it were taken out of context? The vertical slant shows that the writer is poised and in control, yet the high-flying t-bars ("about," "character," "let," and T) indicate a vivid imagination and spirit of adventure. He is as sharp as the needlepointed tops of the small letters. Sometimes he's an impulsive, spur-of-the-moment guy who acts on hunches (breaks within words), but at other times he's capable of constructive planning (good connections, especially between t and o in "to"). The altruistic y in "you" usually appears in a right slant.

If you come to any darling conclusions about my character, let me know!! T.P.

↖ TONY PERKINS

Here's an interesting discrepancy between a signature that is individualistic and hard to decipher and the smaller, regular, easy-to-read text. It is the handwriting of David Soul, whose originally penned signature cries out for recognition of his ability as an independent actor and singer, but whose regular script with its rounded, energetic-pressured regular writing shows that he can follow orders and do a good job as Hutch in the TV series *Starsky and Hutch.* He's not like so many television-series actors who complain about being "locked into a role," although the originality manifested in his writing (look at the unusual capital I as well as the unique signing of his name) prove he can succeed in many other roles—and does. There are no lower zone letters in his name, yet the signature writing dips below the baseline, showing that he can hold his own in an argument if necessary. But the text proves he's easy to get along with, is logical and intuitive, and doesn't possess the great self-confidence he shows the world.

David Soul's own words reinforce what graphology tells us. Just as his signature is inscrutable and spectacular, the body of his writing is clearly readable and simple. He is a down-to-earth guy who can live up to his public image when necessary. While in London to promote his new motion picture, he told a reporter about his luxurious surroundings: "It is not really me, but it is part of the business. It goes with selling the film." And about the adulation that swamps him on both sides of the Atlantic: "You never get used to it. I have to keep a sense of values. It is unnatural to be a 'pop idol, a supercop.' I'm not either of those things. I'm very much a human being. An actor playing a part."

The regular, rather modest and readable script reveals this regular "human being" behind the theatrical mask presented to the world in his indecipherable, flamboyant signature.

If both the text and signature are legible and regular, the writer is uncomplicated and easy to know and understand. The following samples penned by actors Brian Keith and Desi Arnaz Jr. illustrate this. Although both are straightforward, can't you see individual differences? Experienced, versatile Brian Keith is shrewd and intelligent (sharp-pointed letters) and logical (no breaks between letters). Careful i-dots indicate a good memory in remembering lines and the character he is portraying. Leadership is shown in the extended t-bar in "Keith," but he doesn't have the superego that prevents him from doing a fine job in secondary as well as starring roles. Insert Illustration 198 page 251B

Although Desi Arnaz Jr. is much younger and less experienced, he is also logical, with a strong sense of pride, idealism, and self-worth (large capitals). Determination and persistence are proved by the downstroke in D, but he is *not* an arrogant snob. His geniality and good nature appear in the rounded m's and n's and the generously outreaching end-strokes.

the quick brown fox jumped over the whatsis —

Brian Keith

Never grasp after things, least you become attached to them.

Desi Arnaz.

The following handwriting of Anne Baxter is more difficult to decipher, proving that she is more mysterious and complex. Speedy (quick-thinking), unique, and theatrical (original, swirly formations), upslanting (optimistic and ambitious), she is at home in the spotlight. A born actress and individualist, she works hard at anything she undertakes whether it is delineating a role or writing a book. Unlike the unscrupulous ingenue she played in *All About Eve*, Anne would never seek glory at the expense of someone else. She loves people (extreme forward slant) and is altruistic (note the way the g in "stranger" swings to the right of the stem). Some of her ovals are open at the top, others tightly closed, meaning that she is frank and friendly but can be trusted to keep a secret. The looped t-stems mean sensitivity to criticism and the unusual x that becomes part of the t in "Baxter" shows constructive ability and originality. This ultratalented actress will never melt into the crowd.

*Truth is stranger than
fiction — but not so
popular,*

Mark Twain

If you or your lover writes illegibly you have some good
company. Among geniuses of the past who did so is Charles
Dickens, whose tiny, criss-crossy writing was the common
headache of nineteenth-century proofreaders. Thackeray's
penmanship was so microscopic that he once said if he
couldn't sell his stories, he'd make a living writing the Lord's
Prayer on people's thumbnails. Many men of letters had such
illegible scrawls that Hawthorne called illegibility an
"author-like" trait. In fact, many of his own stories, like huge
passages of Shakespeare and Montaigne, still remain un-
published because no one has ever been able to decipher
them!

Balzac's hieroglyphics were so hard on the eyes that the few
printers who could read them had an agreement with the boss
to work on his manuscript only one hour at a time. Carlyle's
crabbed, cramped, erratic writing reflected his gouty nature so
accurately that a proofreader quit his job on *The Edinburgh
Review* and fled Scotland to escape it, only to have his first
"take" in London turn out to be a hectic Carlyle manuscript.
Friends of Victor Hugo compared his writing to a musical
score or a battlefield on paper in which the killed words are
well-stamped-out and the new recruits pushed forward in anything but good order. Twenty-four hours after writing anything, poet Sydney Smith couldn't read his own scrawl, which
he said looked as if "a swarm of ants, escaping from an
ink-bottle, had walked over a sheet of paper without wiping
their legs."

Is your lover's scrawl as confusing as that of Henry Ward
Beecher, who wrote so badly that his daughter used three
guiding rules in copying his manuscripts? (1) If a letter was
dotted, it was *not* an i; (2) if a letter was crossed, it was *not* a

t; and (3) if a word began with a capital letter, it did *not* begin a sentence. Or as enigmatic as the writing of James Joyce whose handwritten manuscript of *Ulysses* was found in the mails by a World War I censor and seized and studied by Britain's best code experts, who were sure it was a dangerous new enemy code?

What about the handwriting of *New York Tribune* editor Horace Greeley, whose notes refusing lectures and social invitations were always misread as enthusiastic acceptances, and whose letters firing employees were used as references to get better jobs. Once he wrote a notation to the *Tribune* painter to make a sign telling the public:

ENTRANCE ON SPRUCE STREET

After hours of trying to figure out the illegible scrawl, the painter thought he'd deciphered it, grabbed his brush and painted this sign, which he posted on the front door of the *Tribune* office:

EDITOR'S ON A SPREE

Napoleon's letters to Josephine were mistaken for rough maps of the battlefield, but he was hot-tempered about other people's handwritings. When he angrily swore at the Las Cases boy for not being able to read a chapter of *The Campaign of Italy*, which he thought the boy had written, he was chagrined to learn that *he* had written the hieroglyphics, which were undecipherable even to himself!

The Duke of Wellington was once involved in a scandal because of another man's unreadable writing. When he was in the House of Lords, the Duke received this letter from J. C. Loudon, the eminent landscape designer and botanist:

> My Lord Duke:
>   It would gratify me extremely if you would permit me to visit Strathfieldsaye at any time convenient to Your Grace to inspect the Waterloo beeches.
>   Your Grace's faithful servant,
>   J. C. Loudon

The Waterloo beeches were trees that had been planted after the Battle of Waterloo to commemorate the great victory, but Loudon's writing was so illegible that Wellington misread not only the contents, but also the signature, which looked like "C. H. London." And so, with his usual dukely promptness and politeness, he responded:

My dear Bishop of London:

It will always give me great pleasure to see you at Strathfield-saye. Pray come there whenever it suits your convenience, whether I am home or not. My servant will receive orders to show you as many pairs of breeches *of mine as you wish; but why you should wish to inspect those that I wore at the Battle of Waterloo is quite beyond the comprehension of*
Yours, most truly,
Wellington.

The good Bishop of London, Blomfield, who hadn't been in touch with Wellington for two years was shocked by this unexpected letter concerning the Duke's trousers. He showed it to the Archbishop of Canterbury and other dignitaries, who shook their heads sadly, fearing the Great Duke had flipped!

All of this is by way of saying that some of the world's great men and women have written illegibly. Before you let yourself be turned off by irregularity or illegibility in a script, check out the other graphological signs, then fit the jigsaw pieces of the puzzle together and see how the total agrees or disagrees with your own personality as it is revealed in your writing.

Remember that negative traits like brutality, dishonesty, egocentricity, dullness, or selfishness may be found in a regular handwriting, whereas wonderful traits like altruism, loving-kindness, consideration, humor, and exciting genius may appear in an irregular one.

Now, before you start going to the other extreme, condemning a highly *regular* hand as bad news, be aware that the man or woman whose handwriting is extremely uniform is not necessarily dull and talentless. In a regular writing, look for some variety and originality, as in the following writing sample:

Build thee more stately mansions, O my soul,
As the swift seasons roll!
Leave thy low-vaulted past!
Let each new temple, nobler than the last,
Shut thee from heaven with a dome more vast,
Till thou at length art free,
Leaving thine outgrown shell by life's unresting sea!

Oliver Wendell Holmes

Or in these highly regular handwritings:

practical—no fantasies

> My father was a hunter all of his adult
> life. But, whereas he would show no emotion
> when shooting a deer to fill our almost empty
> larder, his compassion and love for wild animals
> was among the greatest I have ever known.

musician—writer

> Right now I have to get
> a May 14 program for my
> music club organized, but after
> that why don't we try for another
> Thursday? Even if you haven't
> called me, just drop in. If
> I don't have a supper on hand,
> we can drink tall glasses if

poet

> His droll little mouth was drawn up like a bow;
> And the beard of his chin was as white as the snow;
> The stump of a pipe he held tight in his teeth,
> And the smoke it encircled his head like a wreath;
> He had a broad face and a round little belly,
> That shook when he laughed, like a bowlfull of jelly.
> He was chubby and plump, a right jolly old elf,
> And I laughed when I saw him, in spite of myself;
> A wink of his eye and a twist of his head,
> Soon gave me to know I had nothing to dread;

great poet

> Here is a symbol in which
> Many high tragic Thoughts
> Watch their own eyes.
>
> This gray rock standing tall
> On the headland, where the seawind
> Lets no tree grow,
>
> Earthquake-proved, and signatured
> By ages of storms: on its peak
> A falcon has perched.

socialite

Handwriting Sample and
Excuses for Absences

Now let's see how you analyze the following writing samples on your own. Remember, don't let the first impression of a highly regular or irregular script fool you. Use the skills you've learned in this book to find other character clues within the body of the writing.

Suppose you're a young woman who wants a deep relationship and you have proposals from the following very attractive men who say they love you and want to spend their lives making you happy. Which one would you choose?

Permit me to express to you and all the members of your family my sincere sympathy in this hour of your great bereavement—

Sincerely,
Chas Weidner Jr

Now is the time for all good men, etc.

Georg

There will be legal battles and much pain before it is over. My children are so beautiful and loving I will go to court until I'm 100 in order to keep them.

Now the last time I wrote from Arizona you never answered; please don't let this happen again,

Just couldn't breathe any more, there — even when there wasn't any smog. Had to get out.

The mountains here, and the air, are beautiful. The sunsets stagger the esthetic capacity — every night. And when the moon comes up over the mountain it makes you cry! That's when I think of you.

to be good or lucky. So, somewhere in my mind I am thinking now that I should make my handwriting "good" so you will find good things about me. But I suppose handwriting changes with one's mood or what is affecting me during a given set

Did you choose Number 1? He's logical, emotionally stable, energetic, and dependable. But he's a stickler for convention and you'd have to toe the line. Life with him would be predictable, but perhaps too much so, if you like change and adventure.

Number 2 is a TV director, much sexier than the first, as

you can tell from the long extensions, which are well balanced
by high upper strokes. He is aware of his high position and
abilities and would expect you to be also. He's discriminating
and you should be honored that he approves of you.

Perhaps you chose Number 3. The regularity of his script,
characterized by the rounded shape, emphasis on the middle
zone, upturned finals, and unbroken connections attest to geniality, practicality, loyalty, cheerfulness, and logic. He is so
devoted to his children that you'll never come *first* in his affections although he has enough love and good humor to go
around. If you already have a child from a previous marriage
and are looking for a harmonious family situation, he could be
a good bet. He'll love yours if you love his.

Number 4 is a handsome, personable young man, who is so
affectionate that his emotions often run away with him. In addition to the excessive right slant, the high-flying t-bars
indicate his infinite imagination, and the weak pressure and
short lower loops promise more romantic talk than sexual performance. Weak-willed and overly sympathetic, he soon went
through the vast fortune which he inherited.

Number 5's writing is just as irregular as Number 4's but
what a difference! The dynamic vitality proved by his vigorous
pressure indicates that the irregularity in shape, slant, and
baselines does not mean instability or moodiness but
versatility. He's working hard at several things: acting, direct-
ing, and playwriting. He's much more down-to-earth (lower,
stronger t-crosses, steady connections between letters, and
large middle-zone letters). Although there's occasional irritation (dashed i-dots), the rounded m's and n's show that he's
basically kind-hearted and easy to get along with.

Let's try another. Suppose you're a man who's tired of
one-night stands and who wants a more permanent relationship. First, analyze your own personality and needs. Then
decide the type of woman you would choose from the handwritings of these four very attractive, popular girls:

HOPE ALL IS WELL WITH
YOU — YOU'RE INSPIRING A NEW
BATCH OF "BUDDING" WRITERS, I
KNOW — YOU CERTAINLY CHANGED
MY LIFE — ENRICHED IT — FOR
WHAT THAT'S WORTH. I ALWAYS

I am a woman of many faces — one day a
cherub, the next day a mischievous imp and on some
days, an absolute demon. I bounce
on both ends of the see-saw, for it is either too
hot or too cold, too high or too low, too long or
too short. My Scorpion traits are difficult to conceal
from any astute observer.

My friend, Judy, is the only true blonde
I know. How refreshing it is to see
her and not have to think, "Does she
or doesn't she?" I have had the pleasure of her friendship for years . . . .
in fact, dating back to kindergarten.
Our high school years were really
fun. She used to laugh and "cut-up"
(Please)

Here's the sample of my handwriting you
asked for. Let this also serve as my
release that you may do with this whatever you please.

If you chose woman number 1 you'd have a brilliant, intuitive partner, entirely in control of her emotions. Not a flaming
passionflower unless you . . .

Lady number 2 is a regular writer who is NOT as
many-faced as she claims to be. The smallness, clarity, and
consistency of the words plus the agreeably rounded forms
prove that she is affable, has great powers of concentration
and logic. She isn't even upsettingly moody or she wouldn't
write such straight baselines!

Numbers 3 and 4 are more flamboyant and colorful. Both are
beautiful actresses and affectionate extroverts; the first will
keep your life exciting because of the many contradictions in
her nature. The long, swinging beginning strokes show
dependence and a need to lean on her man, but the low-flung

finals and lofty capitals show pride and a desire to have her own way. The enormous lower loops show a strong interest in the physical and material, but she's also intelligent, logical, and practical.

Girl number 4 is an ultrabeautiful, charming girl who attracts men but is very discreet and discriminating about her friends and activities. Clear thinking ability is proved by the lack of intertangled lines and loops; her need to be alone occasionally, by the spaces between words; and her agreeableness and eagerness to please, by the rounded m's and n's.

How did you fare? Were you able to select the lover or lovers who were best suited to your personality? If not, reread the book and practice your skills on the handwriting of friends and relatives. Then, when you feel confident enough, you'll be ready to apply them to the handwriting of potential lovers.

If you'd like counseling before committing yourself on love or marriage, seek someone who is as wise, compassionate, helpful, and sympathetic as the brilliant young rabbi whose handwriting is shown below. His inclined slant in a gracefully formed, easy-to-read script shows that he loves people and understands their emotions and problems. The extended finals mean that he's generous with his knowledge and time. He isn't critical or judgmental, but totally understanding. The excellent spacing and consistent connections indicate high intelligence, and the rounded m's and n's are signs of amiability, although his closed a's and o's prove that he can be trusted to keep your confidence and not reveal your secrets—ever! He is a well-organized person, both mentally and physically.

Graphology can not only help you choose the right partner, but also the right consultant. Do not pour out your problems, doubts, and emotions to someone who is prejudiced, cold, or who may wisecrack, as some lovelorn columnists are inclined to do. Try to know your adviser through his or her handwriting. Study it for the indications of compassion, understanding, clear, logical thinking, and vigorous life-loving that appear in the script of the rabbi and also in that of the minister in Chapter 13 and the priest in Chapter 5.

"He who has a choice has trouble," says an old Dutch proverb. But this doesn't have to be true in the all-important decision you make in selecting a lover or lifemate. This may be the most important step you'll ever take, so be sure to give it at least as much thought as you give to buying a house or a car—which you can more easily dispose of, if necessary.

Remember also, in all human contacts, to be more concerned with true character than external appearance. Jean Paul Richter wrote: "A person never discloses his own character as clearly as when he describes another's."

You might add "or when he reveals it in handwriting."

18.
Date or Mate Trait List

> Our virtues are learned at mother's knee; vices at some other joint.
>
> —Anonymous

Will what turns you on about a person eventually turn you off? Here's how to double-check for specific traits. Ask yourself: *Is your lover (are you)* . . . ?

Absentminded: omitted i-dots and t-bars; repeated letters or words.

Acquisitive (greedy): crowded letters and words; no margins; short terminals; beginning hooks.

Active: heavy pressure; firm downstrokes; fast speed; angular form; post-placed t-bars and i-dots.

Adaptable: round forms; garland connections; even pressure; medium capitals.

Aesthetic (cultured): well-proportioned, graceful letters (especially capitals); wide margins and well-proportioned spacing; Greek d and g.

Affected (phony): large, flourished capitals and loop extensions; strange arcade shape.

Affectionate, amorous: right slant; long lower loops; heavy pressure.

Aggressive: angular script; heavy pressure; fast speed; extra-strong t-bars (may slant downward) (see Chapter 8).

Agitated (irritable): dash-like i-dots; changing slant, shape, and pressure; jerky connections.

Alcoholic: thick rough form; filled-in heavy lower loops; downhill baselines; shaky connections.

Altruistic: return strokes of lower loops swing right without crossing the stem; script is all or partially rounded; capitals joined to following letters.

Ambiguous: loops of one line tangling with line above or below.

Ambitious: ascending baselines and t-crosses; fast speed; even pressure; large capitals; long upper and lower extensions.

Amiable: right-slanted, rounded writing; garland connections; m's and n's look like u's and w's; upward endstrokes (see Chapter 8).

Amoral: illegible script; wrong or no punctuation or letter forms.

Apprehensive: broken upper and lower loops; backturns in forward or vertical script; weak pressure and t-bars.

Ardent: see Affectionate (see also Chapters 4, 5, and 6).

Arrogant: lofty capitals, especially I; first stroke of capital M very high (see Chapter 9).

Aspiring: high, pointed upper loops; ascending t-crosses; light-to-medium pressure.

Assertive: enormous capitals; open ovals; down-flung terminals and t-bars (see Chapter 9).

Audacious: large, heavy "Look at me!" script; wide connecting strokes; club-thick terminals; long firm t-bars.

Beneficent: see Altruistic.

Broad-minded: well-spaced words and lines; at least some rounded letters; uniformity of pressure and size (capital I's not too high) (see Chapter 13).

Calm: low, unspectacular round i-dots and normal t-bars.

Capricious: varying slant, pressure, and size; convex baselines; concave saucer-shaped t-crosses.

Careful: legible, medium-sized script; even pressure and margins; normal t-bars and i-dots; closed ovals.

Careless: illegible; omitted i-dots and t-crosses; uneven pressure.

Carnal (licentious): thick, crude script with upper and lower loops overlapping.

Cautious: light, preplaced t-bars and i-dots; closed

ovals; accented punctuation; no flourishes or exaggerations; usually vertical slant.

Changeable (vacillating): shifting slant, size, and/or pressure.

Clear-thinking: legible, well-spaced words and lines with no confusing entanglements with lines above and below; well-connected letters in each word.

Coarse (crude): smeary writing with filled-in loops and ovals; heavy, ungraceful pressure; illegible.

Cold-hearted: sharp, rigid, angular backhand slant (unless person is left-handed) (see Chapters 6 and 8).

Conceited: huge I and other capitals; inflated upper loops; triangular lower loops; looped beginning strokes (see Chapter 9).

Concentrate (able to): small, clear writing with low, round i-dots; short upper and lower extensions (see Chapter 9).

Conscientious: straight baselines; open ovals; correctly placed (round) i-dots.

Constructive: original forms; unique, versatile letters and word connections; printlike letters; interesting connections between words such as an i-dot or t-cross joining the next word.

Contemplative: low t-bars and i-dots; small writing, backward slant; upper extensions larger than the lower ones (see Chapter 9).

Conventional: copybook letter forms; medium size; consistently even margins.

Cooperative: rounded form; legible signature that matches the writing in the contents of the letter (see Chapter 8).

Courageous: firm, heavy pressure and t-bars; concave or straight baselines; strokes heavier toward the end; wide spacing (see Chapter 5).

Creative: clever, original, versatile formations; letter g like number 8.

Critical: tent-shaped i-dots; knife-sharp, pointed letters and strokes.

Cruel: heavy t-bars (may slash downward); extra-strong i-dots and descending terminals (see Chapter 14); strong angular shape with no rounded forms; clawlike hooks.

Cultured: see Aesthetic.

Cunning: words tapering until the last letters are sinuous and ambiguous.

Curious: high, round i-dots and letters in the middle zone pointed at the top.

Deceitful: closed, looped ovals, snaky baseline; ambiguous, sinuous word forms (see Chapter 14).

Demonstrative: many flourishes; right slant; high, dashed, or curled t-bars; open ovals; heavy pressure; fast speed or tempo.

Dependable: arrow-straight lines; regularity of slant, size, and pressure.

Depressed or *Despondent:* descending baselines; light (descending) t-crosses (see Chapter 7).

Determined: long, heavy t-bars; lower extensions are strong, straight lines instead of loops; angular-shaped words.

Diffident: very low capitals; light pressure and t-crosses.

Dignified: tall, angular capitals; firm downstrokes.

Diplomatic: words tapering to a thin line; closed ovals.

Direct: no beginning strokes; short endstrokes; simple forms; t-bars to the right of the stem.

Dishonest: see Deceitful (see also Chapter 14).

Dominating: towering capitals; heavy, long hooks or downslanting t-bars.

Dull: all letters extremely rounded in a generally large copybook script; all letters connected with absolutely no breaks and no originality or variation in forms.

Eccentric: bizarre, grotesque forms that may be scrolls, strange loops, triangles, and circles; illegible signature and script.

Economical: closely cramped letters and words; omitted or narrow margins or left margin narrowing as the lines proceed; omitted or short finals (see Chapter 10).

Egotistical: see Conceited.

Energetic: heavy pressure; firm downstrokes; angular form (see Chapter 5).

Enthusiastic: long, high t-bars; ascending baselines; moderate to heavy pressure.

Exaggerates: large writing with many flourishes; extremely wide upper and lower loops; ultrawide margins (see Chapter 9).

Excitable: high t-bars and i-dots; uneven irregular pressure and changing slant.

Extravagant: extrawide margins and spaces between words; large writing (see Chapter 10).

Extroverted: rightward slant; rounded, garland, or a mixture of the two (see Chapters 6 and 8).

Fastidious: low, round i-dots; small writing with light pressure; a meticulous, easy-to-read script.

Fearful: light or weakening pressure; short, feeble t-crosses; breaks in upstrokes of upper-zone extensions.

Feeble: shaky, tremulous form; light pressure (especially downstrokes); broken or bent strokes (see Chapter 5).

Fickle: vacillating slant and pressure (see Capricious).

Flirtatious: finals and tops of letters fly up in the air like flags.

Fluent talker: looped t's and d's; open ovals.

Frank: open a's and o's; letters do not dwindle at the end of a word; in fact, they usually get larger.

Friendly: wide, garland connections; rounded letters; right slant; extended finals (see Chapter 8).

Frugal: see Economical (see also Chapters 6 and 8).

Frustrated: knotted ovals; incompleted lower loops; encircled signature (see Chapter 4).

Generous: extended or ascending finals; wideness of words and spaces between them; y's, g's, and f's lower extension returns to right of stem (see Chapter 10).

Gentle: letters round or garlanded; pressure not too heavy.

Greedy: see Acquisitive.

Honest: spontaneous, legible script; open a's and o's (see Chapter 14).

Hopeful: upturned finals; ascending baseline (see Chapter 7).

Humorous: curvy, smile-shaped i-dots; wavy t-bars, and other graceful curves.

Hypocritical: a's and o's open at bottom and/or knotted at top; crooked baseline letters tapering down from large to small or thin line.

Idealistic: high, light t-bars and i-dots; up-curved terminals (especially d which flies upward); long, pointed upper loops.

Imaginative: extremely high-flying t-bars and i-dots; tall upper extensions.

Impatient: excessive speed so that letters aren't carefully formed; dashed i-dots; very long, thin t-crosses; uneven pressure.

Impulsive: fast speed; t-bars and i-dots to the right; many breaks between letters.

Inactive: slow, rounded forms; faint pressure; uneven spacing.

Inattentive: omitted or high-dashed i-dots; large, varying slant.

Indecisive: backhand or varying slant; wavy baseline; small, soft letter forms; weak t-bars (usually preplaced, as are the i-dots); saucer-shaped t-crosses.

Independent: large capitals but short d-stems; high first strokes of m, n, and w.

Indifferent: very reclined or vertical.

Ingenious: legible, versatile writing usually print-shaped and original; open ovals; ascending baseline.

Intelligent: superior forms without beginning strokes or flourishes; well-spaced, small, clear writing with a good balance of breaks and good connections between letters; consistency between text and signature; g like number 8.

Intense: very heavy pressure in downstrokes.

Introverted: always writes a small, narrow, cramped backhand; convex t-crosses; signature and envelope address left of center (see Chapter 9).

Intuitive: broken letter connections in a superior script; fairly tall upper extensions, t-bars, and i-dots (see Chapter 13).

Inventive: unusual connections, especially between words, for instance, a t-bar or i-dot joins with the next word; first and last names may also be joined; fluid script (see Chapter 13).

Irritable: sharp, heavy, angular writing; long, heavy, or clublike t-bars; heavy, dashed i-dots; knife-sharp finals (see Chapter 8).

Jealous: extreme backhand; heavy or uneven pressure; incurving hooks on t-bars or finals; overscored signature; too-high t-bars.

Kind: right-slanted round writing with garlands; ascending terminals; legible, pleasing to read, without sharp pointed strokes (see Chapters 6 and 8).

Lazy: see Inactive.

Logical: excellent connections; consistent slant, shape, and pressure (see Chapter 13).

Loyal: extremely legible (especially signature); open a's and o's; consistent slant.

Luxury-loving: large, flourished capitals; wide spaces and margins; huge script.

Malicious: down-slanting t-bars and i-dots; angle-shaped i-dots.

Materialistic: thick, heavy pressure; smeared i-dots; inflated lower loops (much larger than the upper extensions).

Melancholy: descending baselines; irregularity; everything seems to pull downward (see Chapter 7).

Miserly: narrow writing; no margins or wide spacing between words; short, hooked finals (see Chapter 10).

Moderate: medium size and pressure; signature matches writing in text; lacks exaggerated loops, especially upper.

Modest: unostentatious script with small, medium capitals (especially I; unflourished, simple signature; see Chapter 9).

Narrow-minded: crowded letters and words; no extended terminals (see Chapter 13).

Nervous: small, shaky letters with uneven pressure; jerky connections; many retouches.

Nonconforming: may be illegible but superior form; angular; may change slant (plus other defiance of traditional rules).

Observant: small, clear writing with sharp, angular tops on many of the small letters.

Obstinate: heavy pressure; angular script; thick t-bars that are either hooked, down-flung; rightward slant makes sudden left turns.

Opinionated: huge capitals (especially I); inflated upper extensions; strong downstrokes.

Optimistic: ascending baselines and finals.

Orderly: neat, regular form; even margins; round, correctly placed i-dots; good punctuation; legible.

Original: see Inventive.

Particular: emphasized, low, round i-dots; envelope address descends in neat steps.

Passionate: see Affectionate; Amorous (see also Chapter 4).

Patient: precisely even, well-placed t-bars; low, round i-dots; slow speed; at least some rounded forms; light to medium pressure.

Perceptive: see Observant.

Persevering and *Persistent:* level baselines; even pressure; strong downstrokes (often with hooks at the end); good connections; strong t-bars (sometimes hooked or connected to the next word).

Poised: unchanging vertical slant; proudly tall but un-flourished capitals.

Practical: long lower and short upper loops; narrow margins; medium size and pressure; omitted or short terminals.

Procrastinating: t-bars and i-dots to the left of the stem; slow speed.

Pugnacious: heavy, hasty, usually backhand writing with heavy finals and t-bars that slash downward; angular writing and i-dots.

Reasonable: see Logical.

Refined: light, small, well-formed letters; high t-bars and i-dots.

Resentful: firm beginning strokes start below the baseline; sharply pointed letters.

Reserved: small or medium-small reclined slant; closed a's and o's; modest capitals (especially I); under-scored or encircled signature.

Restless: see Nervous.

Secretive: closed, looped o's, a's, and d's; extreme backhand; almost illegible signature.

Self-confident: tall but simply formed capitals; un-flourished signature.

Self-controlled: vertical slant; convex t-bars; straight baseline; good spacing; legible.

Selfish: in-curved finals or those with a strong hook; middle zone larger than upper or lower; underscored *and* overscored signature (see Chapter 11).

Self-protective: final stroke of the signature circles over the name; signature is fully encircled (see Chapter 11).

Sensitive: upper stroke of small letter d is an inflated loop; also looped t-stems.

Sensuous: heavy pressure; extreme right slant; muddy i-dots and large ink-filled lower loops.

Shallow: curled snail-shell lower loops throughout script; middle-zone letters larger than upper or lower.

Shrewd: sharp, angular forms; closed ovals; letter

dwindling at the end of words; short finals (see Chapter 8).

Sincere: straight baselines; open ovals; right slant; legible script.

Snobbish: flourishes throughout; extra-wide left margins; tall capitals (especially I).

Sociable: round and scalloped forms, clear, readable script (see Chapter 8).

Spiritual: light pressure; upper extension letters predominate; upturned terminals.

Stable: vertical or slight slant either way; even pressure, slant, and shapes of letters; normal i-dots and t-bars. See Poise.

Stingy: no final strokes or spaces between words; crowded, angular writing (see Chapter 10).

Stupid: slow speed; many pauses and touched-up letters; excessive roundness; childishly awkward forms; many flourishes and ornate strokes.

Submissive: light, low, short t-bars; light pressure; low capitals; monotonous roundness; small writing.

Suicidal: final strokes slash leftward, canceling out what has been written (especially the signature); a strong downward pull to the whole script and signature; writing tends to favor the lower left-hand part of the page.

Superficial: saucer-shaped t-bars; wavy underscoring of the signature.

Tactful: a tapering of the size of the letter at the end of word; closed ovals; neat, balanced margins and script; often a left-slanting writing.

Tactless: letters get larger at the end of a word; a's and o's are wide open at the tops; short, abrupt finals; t-crosses to the right of the stem; very narrow or no margins.

Tenacious: t-crosses and finals end with a fishhook; angular form.

Tense: see Nervous.

Timid: see Submissive.

Vacillating: mixed slant, pressure and/or size; t-crosses are saucer-shaped or preplaced (to left of stem).

Vain: see Conceited (see also Chapter 9).

Versatile: an interesting variety in the way the same letters are formed; intuitive breaks between letters; changing slant in a superior writing.

Violent: pasty, thick writing; threatening t-bars that resemble clubs; heavy and down-slashing; extra-thick downstrokes (see Chapter 14).

Vital: firm but clear, heavy script (often large); quick pace; long extensions in the lower zone; post-placed i-dots and t-bars (see Chapter 5).

Vivacious: ascending baselines and finals; i-dots and t-bars fairly high and gracefully dashed or wavy.

Vulgar: hideous, illegible, or almost illegible, heavy, smudged forms; ink-filled loops; too-strong lower and upper strokes; clublike forms and curlicues (see Coarse).

Weak-willed: extremely light t-bars and i-dots; irregular slant in a very weak-pressured script.

Zealous, zestful, or *zippy:* high, right-placed t-bars and i-dots in a fluid, fast-moving script; moderately heavy to heavy pressure; some angular letters (although they may alternate with garlanded and a very few rounded ones) (see Chapters 5 and 8).

If the qualities you are looking for in a lover aren't included in this list, try synonyms for those qualities or think about the ingredients that make up that characteristic. It's impossible to include *every* trait, but throughout the book you will probably find clues to those that are important in your love relationships.

Books You'll Enjoy from SIGNET

☐ **INSIDE INTUITION: What We Know About Nonverbal Communication by Flora Davis.** Everything BODY LANGUAGE didn't tell you about how you can read a person like a book! After reading this book, you will know how to *watch* as well as listen to others in order to get their true message. (#J7831—$1.95)

☐ **FACE READING by Timothy T. Mar.** Every person's character is clearly written all over his or her face—*if you know what vital checkpoints to look for!* After reading this fascinating work, you will become expert at unmasking "false faces" to get at the true character of any person— in your work life, your social life, your sex life. Here is a unique skill that can change the face of your own life! (#W6539—$1.50)

☐ **SUCCESS THROUGH TRANSACTIONAL ANALYSIS by Jut Meininger with a Foreword by Robert L. Goulding, M.D.** Here is the book that shows you exactly how you are interacting with others, what secret goals and desires are driving you, and how to understand the actions of those around you. This is the breakthrough book that makes I'M OK—YOU'RE OK work for you! (#E7840—$1.75)

☐ **LOVE AND ADDICTION by Stanton Peele with Archie Brodsky.** This provocative book focuses on interpersonal relationships to explore what addiction really is—psychologically, socially, and culturally. "A rare book, like FUTURE SHOCK and THE PURSUIT OF LONELINESS, that is destined to become a classic!"—*Psychology Today* (#E6985—$2.25)

☐ **LOVE, SEX, AND SELF-FULFILLMENT: Keys to Successful Living by Martin Grossack, Ph.D.** This inspiring book, by one of the leading disciples of Dr. Albert Ellis's Rational Emotive Therapy, shows you how to know who you really are and feel good about it, be open and free in your sexual life, and much more. (#W8021—$1.50)

To order these titles, please

use coupon on next page.

Recommended Reading from SIGNET